9:11
THE HOUSE OF STEEL

By Chris Ibanez

With I. Flores

To: Robert Earl

Love Hope aka Peanuts

"All authority in heaven and on earth has been given to Me. Therefore go and make disciples of all nations, baptizing them in the name of the Father and of the Son and of the Holy Spirit, and teaching them to obey everything I have commanded you. And surely I am with you always, to the very end of the age."

Jesus Christ

All our hands give You, Lord, our whole heart. We adore You and honor Your love and friendship. We kneel always at Your feet, where we will forever worship You. To Peanuts, thank you, your heart is beautiful, and I will always cherish our friendship.

Table of Contents

Figure 1: "Crown of Thorns" by Christie Koppel

1

All around evil was operating in ways that only happened on Hollywood big-screens, performed by award winning actors. My heart was salivating in sin, my home a den of darkness where voodoo black magic was practiced. People were going crazy, fish in an aquarium were instruments of sorcery, evil spirits lurked about, demon possession of women happened, and children, people and love were used for weapons to carry out schemes of a hidden world with a dark agenda. Demons were many, and spooky occurrences happened. Large cats, by the dozens, surrounded the house, meowing. At the time, it was the "year of the tiger," according to the Chinese zodiac.

Life was confused, the heart in a horrible condition and a Mount Everest of challenge was unfolding. A single step in the wrong place, in any direction, and federal officials from the United States Homeland Security Immigrations Customs Enforcement (ICE) would have been there with a shiny pair of handcuffs and enough evidence to make a 20-year prison sentence stick. All my steps were ordained the moment a decision was made to walk away from a criminal life, a life full of every sensual addiction. By this point, the United States Justice department had plagued my life for over two years, poking around and kicking rocks over.

In January 2014, a federal grand jury released ten criminal indictments, and I found myself caught in the middle of a million-dollar international drug smuggling conspiracy that stretched from California, Minnesota, Hawaii, and to Guam. The investigation involved the highest level of state and federal law enforcement officials, from state police to DEA and Homeland Security Immigrations Customs Enforcement. Three hundred arrests, across 13 street gangs, were made in what was dubbed by the United States district attorney as the "Crystal Palace I and II" take down. Weapons, money, and drugs connected to super-labs run by the Mexican drug cartel were seized. As part of "Crystal Palace II," I was indicted for conspiracy to distribute crystal methamphetamines, listed as a fugitive of the law, and arrested by

Immigration Customs Enforcement officials. I was in a mess, in very big trouble, and only an act of God could save me at this point.

Needless to say, I found myself in a house of steel, a federal detention facility, and confronted by gangs that dominate the federal correctional system. Throughout the case, in and out of jail, the lead investigator sent wave after wave of Blue-Shoes[1] operatives to try and obtain incriminating testimony or evidence that would link me to a criminal network. They invaded my world with trickery, entrapments, and insult. Blue-Shoes tried hard, using every deceptive trick in the book of black lies to seal a criminal confession.

And then, it was show-time in the courtroom after two years in the house of steel. The deck was stacked against me. The last thing anybody wanted was truth. They wanted a conviction and would do anything for it to happen. The lead investigator in the case was fabricating evidence throughout the whole process. Every witness testifying in the case lied, informants that cut deals with the law lied, and individuals on wiretaps were reading scripted lines

[1] *Blue-Shoes are individuals affiliated with law enforcement, including informants working both sides of the Law.*

from an award-winning director of lies! Financial records of five years and all money received from anyone, every nickel, dime and dollar were summed to make it look like I was a drug dealer high up in the ranks in control of large sums of cash. The district attorney and his army of assistants were trying a case built on a foundation of lies. At a 98.1% conviction rate that the federal judicial system holds, no one gets away from their grip. It was inevitable, that retirement in the cold house of steel and concrete dungeon of prison was coming and only a miracle could get me out of the trouble that I was in. And on February 29, 2016, at 2:27 pm, twenty-five months after being arrested, the jury announced its verdict.

The criminal trial was the most intense experience in life that was ever faced. The day before jury deliberations began, everything was surreal. The world seemed to be a weight pressing on my shoulders, the silence was imposing, the time intense. Life came to a standstill, and the cold house of steel I was used to had suddenly become a deep freeze. As the marshals searched my body, their hands felt like they were intrusively going through the inner folds of my heart. Everything was penetrating, intensely deep. I felt like a speck of dust in a very large world that was closing in or going further away, I could not tell. The marshals shackled one ankle at a time, the iron jewelry freezing, and every click of the locking mechanism hurt. To move a ligament, painful. Then, the 7-inch nails being hammered through Jesus' feet were thought of, a pain unimaginable and indescribable. For me!

The marshals proceeded to put handcuffs on, while I thought of how Lord Jesus kept silent all the way to the cross with my sins on Him while being beaten and mocked, onlookers yelling murder Him, murder Him! The marshals were sure to tightly fasten the handcuffs around each wrist. The steel was cold, the pain intense and throbbing, as I thought of the indescribable horror the Lord felt as the nails were driven into His wrists. All for me! What Jesus Christ went through on the cross became very personal, profoundly real. Nails penetrated my heart as I remembered a life of sin and what was done to save me. It is a miracle to be alive today. And a miracle can be said a thousand times over for so many Divine acts of intervention that have happened. That I am alive and healthy rather than dead or insane from all the drugs that went into my body is miraculous. In the wake of a life-long struggle with drugs, the destruction can be seen on many levels, on so many fronts in my own life and the thousands met in the journey through the shadows, dark rooms, and gravestones.

In my 40-year struggle with drugs, so much has happened in life. Having the first marijuana cigarette at age 9, drugs plagued my life since. In my journey throughout the world into island extremes and nationwide euphoric escapades that span America, broken homes, families, lives and hurting people and children have been seen. Parents have been watched getting high in front of children, and children getting high on the drugs their parents sold. Children, of friends and family, have been born high with the same crystal meth that went into my veins. I have been the pallbearer for friends who died in labs that made the crystal meth that poisoned my body, destroyed my life and others too numerous to count. And I have seen suicides, murders, and violence caused by the same crystal methamphetamines that filled my veins to numb the mind and escape the reality of my shame. It did not work. I was howling, deeply grieving, and knew no way out. Addiction had now become atypical and extreme. The flirt with death constant, even encouraged. Drunkenness of every sort and extreme to blind my reality and lost life led to the discovery and opening of doors into further darkness and evil: Money, sex, and orgies with the devil!

2

"For our struggle is not against flesh and blood, but against the rulers, against the authorities, against powers of this dark world and against the spiritual forces of evil in the heavenly realms."

Paul of Tarsus

In my home in San Diego, California, happy little boy's feet playfully roamed the hallways. This is a dark spirit in the guise of happy feet that a roommate consulted with to carry out evil agendas that were intended to entrap. The roommate had a legion of dark enterprising spirits that had all kinds of schemes going on and would perform nightly chants in smoke and complete darkness during midnight hours. Many cats would invade the house, it was the year of the tiger according to the Chinese zodiac at the time, and the

roommate's girlfriend is nick-named "Kitty." These were not coincidental occurrences but intentional practices of the roommate and his dark schemes.

One day an aquarium with five unusual looking fish was brought home. Knowing the lengths the roommate and his demonic doings would go, I could not help but wonder what he had in mind with the fish that were much harmless than the cats and required no cooking by a sashimi, fish eating lover that I was! The fish were remarkably beautiful. One night the aquarium water turned silvery-white then blood-red not five hours after the roommate cleaned it. Staring at the fish tank, pondering what was happening, and convincing myself that it was not because I was hallucinating from being high on meth and awake for many days, a story behind the fish began to emerge.

There was an albino, prehistoric looking fish with skeletal looking fingers named "The Sorcerer," a key player in the ring of black magic. There were two black and white orca-looking catfishes that represented my wife and roommate who were fooling around. Since I was known as "The Dragon," a big fiery dragon fish was me. The roommate got its eyes gorged out. Creatures with no eyes are considered soul-less. I remember thinking that it was bad enough to be half blind and cross-eyed from birth and now there are voodoo dances not around a camp fire but a fish tank with a fiery fish, with chants for me, the dragon, to be completely blind and soul-less too! The last fish was called "The Spy" because it just watched and never moved, and it represented a demon possessed girlfriend of the roommate that always wanted to have sex. She was admitted into a crazy hospital for the many voices that were in her. Visiting her at the hospital, she was asked when the voices started and she said that my roommate and his best friend put something evil in her!

Soon, crazier things began to happen in the home. The wife would start a fight out of nowhere, out of nothing, and physical features on her face would change when this happened. Her face would begin an elongation process, eyes would become sunken in, big, round and protruding, and her whole face looking demon like. I remember thinking this is just perfect. Everybody thought I was paranoid when told about an undercover police presence invading my life, that I was crazy when all were told about the voodoo black magic practices of the roommate with fish and cats, and now they were sure to think I went over the deep end if told about something that was only seen on a Hollywood big screen series of the walking dead!

During this period, the wife consumed a half bottle of GNC urinary tract cleaner and a gallon of water in an attempt to get a negative drug test but instead drowned herself and landed in the hospital having life-saving procedures done to save her! She gradually came back to life in eight hours, turning from a pale lifeless block of ice to not only a warm body with a complexion but also a fire breathing mouth that spoke evil. When she regained consciousness, she told everybody that I tried to kill her!

3

"And, behold, a woman in the city, which was a sinner, when she knew that Jesus sat at meat in the Pharisee's house, brought an alabaster box of ointment, and stood at His feet behind Him weeping."

Dr. Luke

Trouble all around for the longest time and no place to turn. No matter what direction turned, no satisfaction could be found, no fulfillment. Everywhere, natural, authentic beings, humans, could not be found. In the mirror, no more could the self be seen, only lies and shame, a meaningless existence. In desperation, the Lord was looked to not for a sign to believe, but to show Truth so that the war within would stop and lashings at the world that continually pulled me away into emptiness and shame would cease. I wanted out of the prison of my heart that was

enslaving me to pain, shame, and sin. And Love was the key.

One afternoon while at L&L Hawaiian BBQ in San Diego, California, a place frequented for lunch, the restaurant attendants, with whom there was a good rapport, were told that this was the day that the yellow display surfboard was going to be taken. To my surprise, all the employees ran to the back, and one pokes her head out and says, “The surveillance cameras do not work!” In my mischievous excitement, I went straight for the hanging yellow surfboard. This restaurant was going to be placed on the map of infamy with an evening news headline saying, “Man steals yellow display surfboard for personal home décor item.” Reaching for the board, it is found attached to a cable. Leaving to get a cutter, patrons are found in the restaurant upon my return. While outside waiting for the patrons to leave, an individual kept sticking a pamphlet with the famous bible verse John 3:16 in my face and was being very annoying. This stranger miraculously gets my phone number. That Sunday a text message from the brother is received, saying, “You are invited to a celebration at our church.” “What if you are high?” I asked. “Come as you are” was the reply. As I was, I came to Jesus Christ--High!

This was one year before being arrested for conspiracy to distribute crystal meth amphetamines. At the height of a life of sin, at a time that I was the highest in life, head deep in the filth that money and drugs brought, and a heart heavily laden in despair and a life so broken and seemingly impossible to repair, I arrive at Fuego Dios to attend a ceremony, a celebration, at the church. After taking a rear corner seat, the celebration began. It was a play of the crucifixion and resurrection of Jesus Christ. Up the center aisle, Jesus walked carrying His cross, and there in my shame I stared at Love. Too laden with guilt, I turned away, but whatever direction turned, the man with the cross circled the aisleways of church pews and was somehow always confronting me. At the center, again, on a platform, the man with the cross hung. And there at the foot of the Cross, at the feet of Jesus Christ, I wept, the moment when love touched my heart and a beauty embraced me, when sin, pain, and shame began flowing out in a torrential pour of tears.

One year prior to being arrested, while crystal meth was still being heavily used, I found myself in a home that was full of brothers of faith and where nothing was in English, but Spanish. There was one, only one sign in the whole home that was in English. Awakening early, the chapel was entered alone. And

there, the first thing that catches my eyes is a sign that read, "Now abide by faith, hope and love"(1 Corinthians 13:13). Crying, I knew right then that the Lord was acknowledging that a conscious decision was made to turn away from a life of sin.

Prior to the United States justice department issuing a federal warrant for my arrest, the state of California had also charged me with eight other felony counts that carried a minimum of three years' incarceration each. The day this trial was to start, while standing before the judge, God spoke to me, while in the background the state judge could faintly be heard dismissing all eight felony counts. It was a surreal moment. What was louder than the judge was the voice of the Lord, not condemning, but gently speaking of the extent of hurt caused to myself, the family, and to all who dearly cared for me. This was a powerful moment of my broken existence and life long struggle with drugs. Tears flowed heavily the whole day, and the eight miracles that happened were not even recognized.

"Woe to those who rise early in the morning to run after their drinks, who stay up late at night till they are inflamed with wine."

Isaiah, The Prophet

There was a time when sex, drugs, and money were the 24-hour lifecycle for more than two years. The thirst for wealth borne all kinds of evil that entangled and enslaved my life, and I knew no way out of the pit of darkness that was being salivated in. The heart was bleeding profusely from pain and shame, to even reach for life there was no desire. Divine intervention was required to walk with confidence again. Proverbs 9 states, "Stolen water is sweet; food eaten in secret is delicious!" This is where the living dead reside, guests in the realm of the dark. The drugs, the money, the sex, the euphoric escapism, the orgies with the devil brought cosmic pleasures but deep within life was becoming emptier and emptier, becoming more lost in a world that was having its way with me.

Although marriage represented many beautiful experiences, such as family and meaningful relationships, it did perpetuate the desires and passions of the flesh. Intimacy and passion were confused and the fire soon died and the wife as a sexual partner became no longer satisfying and extramarital affairs happened. To remove inhibitions, drug use intensified and addiction dangerously went into the extreme deadly abuser. There was a time that the wife and I consumed so much cocaine in an hour that the point of overdose was reached, death was in the next breath. We laid there waiting, frozen in euphoria, knowing and expecting death to come, but death never came even though we both knew it should of!

Drugs were always a part of life. At the age of nine, marijuana and alcohol had already been tried. From this point to age 51, five consecutive years of sobriety time have not been seen. When my oldest son was six months old, the wife and I accidentally got him high when we rolled the windows up in the car while smoking a marijuana cigarette, hot-boxing our son and not even knowing it. When the daughter was three years old, she was picked up while high. Looking into my eyes, she knew something was wrong. This scared her. My youngest son, who is a nephew that the wife and I acquired at two weeks old, was born high on crystal methamphetamines. At the height of our drug addiction, the wife and I were required to take a drug test by a social worker who was concerned for the welfare of our nephew. And to avoid a positive drug test, the wife took some home remedy to cleanse her urinary tract and accidentally drowned herself right before my nephew who called 911. The wife died and was brought back to life by four doctors while my nephew and I watched her turn from a cold block of ice to a warm body with a complexion again.

There have been many intense trips on drugs, so intense that it would make Timothy Leary look like a pothead rather than the founder of the psychedelic acid trip of the 1960s. There were many times when massive amounts of crystal meth were consumed through capsules for twelve or more days to deprive the body of sleep to hallucinate so that everything would become increasingly trance-like. When the body would finally sleep, there were massive occurrences of neuro-electrical short-circuits of synapse nerve ending explosions that sent full body jolts with every explosion of doomed brain cells, sometimes as many as one hundred simultaneous jolts in less than a minute!

In the latter stage of my addiction, use got dangerously intense and heavy, access to crystal meth was virtually unlimited and abundant, and life had fallen apart. Already the marriage and family were gone, financial resources depleted, the search for meaningful employment forgotten, and the will to live, gone. Feeling disowned and abandoned, I called my daughter, telling myself that if she did not answer, a syringe was going to be filled with enough crystal meth to take my life. My daughter would be playing Russian roulette with her father and not even know it. She was called and no answer, nothing happened. Strapping my arm with a belt to expose a vein, the needle was injected and as the syringe plunger began its journey down to deliver death, my phone vibrates atop the bathroom counter. It was a video message from my daughter and granddaughter, one saying "Daddy, I love you" and the other, "Poppa, I love you." I cried, wept deeply in my cowardice shame. This was the first of the series of miracles that began my intrigue of the all-knowing God "out-there."

Although the euphoric escapades that drugs offered needed hard removed from my life, it did not disappear that readily even though it desperately needed to. If it was not one kind of substance, it was another. From the psychedelics and synthetics of the streets to the endless strengths of pharmaceuticals, every type of substance had its time in my life. As substance continued to fill the body with poison anyway I would let it, sin, too, began to take its toll on the heart. Like the Israelites who were enslaved in Egypt, I, too, was a slave to crystal meth and all the sensual pleasures it brought. But after the first miracle when the Lord intervened before I took my life, a change in direction was sensed even though life was still confused. The lifesaving miracle initiated the first steps out of enslavement and into a clearing as the unravelling of my life began to shatter me. I desperately tried to hold on to life as it was, and went to great lengths to preserve my addiction, doing anything to stay high, even if that meant getting all that threatened my lifestyle addicted to crystal meth too.

The push into my clearing was hard and strong, for Blue-Shoes had frozen all assets, blocked movement of all financial resources, and all areas were surveilled to box me in and expose all possible connections that may link me to a criminal network. On Monday, February 7, 2014, United States Homeland Security officials stormed my residence. The United States Justice department was calling my name, hard and very loud. Handcuffed and gagged through constitutional Miranda Rights, I was arrested for conspiracy to distribute crystal methamphetamines in connection to an international drug smuggling network and handed over to officials at the Federal Metropolitan Correctional Center (MCC) in downtown San Diego, California. With nothing but a positive attitude, the house of steel was entered, a day that marked the beginning of life with a new song that was never known before. I was 49 years old! Officially, these were the first steps into a life clearing, and a

time of supernatural courtship that marked my deliverance out of Egypt, my land of slavery to sex, drugs, and money.

LOVE

4

"Love is never alone
Love is always crowded
Love is the shared self
We can not own our love
And we can not teach our love
The longest breath is
The shortest distance to heaven
The deepest life is love
The deepest love is an embrace
Love is not rest
Love is peace
Love is purpose"

Akiane Kramarik[i]

While sitting in a parenting class in the house of steel, a whirlwind of emotions surfaced as concepts were discussed. Visions of past parental mistakes came to mind, virtually bringing me to tears as the failures of fatherhood were remembered. The one success as a father was intuitive love, that the family was provided

for. This falls too short in the fulfillment of fatherhood requirements because love as an emotional expression is far greater than food for the belly and a roof for shelter.

About the time the parenting class started, a dream of the family happened. The timing was intriguing and peculiar, and strongly suggested it was Divinely generated. In the dream, I was moving out of a prison cell, packing items into a box on my bunk, clearly seeing the furnishings of the room and all was happy and harmonious. Necklaces of sorts were being taken from where they hung and placed into a box. There was a large senior portrait of my daughter that folded into squares. In the dream, it was implied that I could leave. This dream seemed to be saying to let go, to let love go on its way and mend all the pain regarding the family and failures and heartaches of fatherhood that weighed heavy on the heart.

Recalling the dream, I wondered what the Lord was saying. With so many peculiar events happening during unusual times, there were no doubts that a Divine being was speaking, ministering to the heart even during sleep. The family was gone and there was peace with it all. There is, I am sure, much buried pain regarding the family, deeply hidden in the heart someplace. Not to dwell on past mistakes and failures, but it seemed that there is much to be gained from the pain, and the wisdom from reflection was sure to speak about love that perfects all. It's not a matter of over-intellectualizing as someone once said. It is strongly believed that there are truths deeply hidden, many times in selfish rationalizations and euphemisms, that have been used to cover and blind the self from the true motivations of the heart or simply as a coping mechanism to mask pain, hurt, and even failures. If this is the case, then these bondages have driven my life. And until the truth is found, I remained a prisoner.

Freedom is not a place, but a reality. And so, whether behind bars or in the world outside mattered not, for if life was weighed down by sin and the heart afflicted, then I am a prisoner and not truly free. Therefore, the pain and hurt surrounding the family needed to be addressed and the Lord was somehow communicating this through a dream. There was no question that the family was dearly loved and missed, that there were also many failures as a father and husband. But the whole idea about love and what it meant was not lining up with what was happening, for all that were dear had taken an express flight of betrayal and abandonment. Love does not disappear with the delete button of 21st century computer science, at least it did not for me. If love does not disappear, then where does it go if it does not hold together in the good, the bad, and the ugly in life? What about forgiveness? Is this a beautiful word of lip service? Have all been truly forgiven? These questions were pounding hard and deep, and the parenting class was causing me to confront many truths about the pain and hurt surrounding the family.

My greatest fear regarding the family was that the failures of a father and a man would cross generational boundaries and that the dysfunctional cycle that I was raised with and parented by had already passed onto the generation of my children and their children by mere witness and direct experience. Remembering the damage done to the family, I find myself wondering when will the vicious cycle end and how many generations back did it all start? These reflections were deeply grieving, painful. But the Lord was showing that love will transform anything, all my pain, hurt and failures, if I would just trust in its power. Life will always have the good, the bad, and the ugly. But no matter the challenge, love transforms because it is never static or passive but alive and transforming.

Love makes everything beautiful. Love challenges, opens many doors in the heart, opens the eyes to see the very reason for life, and provides security and confidence in uncertain times. It drops the barriers of sin and pain that divide the human heart and opens a path that is free to travel, to wander into new horizons with hope even with the uncertainties of tomorrow. Love gives this confidence, a confidence to be still and know that there is a Divine being in control of life and that there are many reasons for why life unfolds as it does. Life is not perfect but love perfects all.

Looking back into the earliest memories of childhood, expressions of love cannot be found. Intuitive love, that mom and siblings would provide and protect, were recognized. There were never times where love was expressed as an outward emotion, from sibling to another or from parent to child. Violence and anger abounded, however. Childhood was alone, in the tranquility of silence contemplating life and death while kicking sand along the seashore or while making crude toy implements with sticks, stones, and banana tree bark. Early on a Divine being was recognized and involved somehow, even though His substance was not known.

As I contemplated on what lessons were supposed to be learned in the wisdom of love, my reflections evoked powerful emotions as the violence, the dysfunction, and even the terror were remembered as a child. In some crazy way, it is within the chaos, in the in-between moments, where the beauty of life is experienced. Finding fault with significant people in our lives, how they may or may have not hurt us, does not change anything for the pain and the hurt are still very real, the failure still happened. Therefore, I have chosen to focus on all that could possibly be learned from every type of experience in life so that I own everything that has happened to me. There are lessons in all experience, our treasures to live by.

As children, all of us wanted to express ourselves to someone significant, a parent, a mother or father figure, so they would attend to us. In what we did with art, the games we played at birthday parties, and the things we did were primarily motivated to bring attention to us from our parents. The gaze, the voice, the hug, the rolling on the ground in a loving and warm embrace were all different dimensions of love and affection that every child craves. Reflecting upon this brings tears, for I have never known such expressions of love and affection as a child. Is this childhood lost? Maybe, but my tears I feel are beautiful because in my own unique way, I get to experience it all in an abstract, even theoretical crazy way where the imagination can make everything perfect, void of all the pain and violence I have known.

In the middle of flooding emotions, something beautiful was beginning to reveal itself, Divine seeds deeply planted in the heart began to sprout and flourish. Instead of seeking love and affection from parents or significant others who were not there, I sought it with a Divine being that I did not know but somehow knew existed. This was the very beginnings of my relationship with the Lord. He was the phantom Being I played with when insects were chased and ant hills climbed and cried to when bitten all over. He was the Being spoken to during the long beach and nature walks and fishing trips that were taken alone, and the Being impressed with primitive toy implements fashioned out of banana tree leaves and bark. Flappers would be made to pop, a popping sound that I knew reached the heavens. Slings from brown banana tree bark would be fashioned and stones swung in David and Goliath scenes many times the world over, with such power and marksmanship that the stone explodes upon impact of its target. These childhood toys and playground times in a parentless world were not alone, they were with Lord Jesus who was always there. He was the Parent that showed love and affection as I impressed Him with ancient toy implements.

In the parenting class, parenting and love were being compartmentalized in a fruitless secular attempt to quantify parenting to influence positive familial circles. There are no doubts that we must understand the influence of innate male and female traits, and even culture and tradition. Nobody can "know" about everything for every given situation, however. My world shows that no amount of knowledge could have influenced or changed the pain, hurt, and intuitive love felt as the windows of time were looked into. Theory is perfect. Reality is brutal and rudely awakens us. Circumstances just prevented my experience from being different even if the adults in the family knew better. There were just too many variables that had influences. Although there were no outward expressions of love and affection, intuitively love was known amidst violence, fear, and pain that were so much a part of my young life. Any other way that childhood could have been would have weakened the faith I have today.

There are no recipe books for life and parenting. There will be endless curves that life will throw, and there will be numerous failures on many levels and fronts that no amount of education will

prepare anybody for. Only a life lived whole-heartedly that ascribes to the calling of love, open and free, will suffice in a journey of many hills and valleys, joys, and sorrows. And Love will carry us when violations of heart in life leave open wounds that never seem to heal.

5

"Mind is the Master-power that molds and makes, And Man is Mind, and evermore he takes the tool of Thought, and, shaping what he wills, brings forth a thousand joys, a thousand ills: --He thinks in secret, and it comes to pass: Environment is but his looking glass."

James Allen[ii]

At a young age, the first inner battle of morality was when dad was observed with another woman at a hotel not three miles from where we lived. Racing home as fast as an 8-year-old can peddle a bike, mom was told. When dad arrived, mom pulled out a three-foot machete and looked like she was going to perform a circumcision of pop's little peter but in her rage, it looked more like an act of murder was going to happen. The most sacred union between a man and woman was violated as if nothing before my eyes and murder was a very possible consequence. The beauty

of a sacred unity was just replaced with brutality whether all ended in murder or not, shocking my young sense of morality. Trust was shattered, my eyes being opened to the reality of people, that nobody does what they say or even try to fulfill even the smallest of promises. And personally, I am no exception to those who fail to do what they say. In fact, I land at the top of the dung pile of fallen humanity. Whether anybody is justified and warranted an exemption from the pile is beyond me. But I must wonder how truly deep the effects of an adulterous act of my father and killer instinct of my mother at a young age. This is not blame or excuse for personal failures. It is the context of the heart that is examined to explain an inner tremendum that seeks to "see" the clashing, conflicting world of morality.

Looking back in the extra-marital affairs in my own marriage, I cannot appreciate the emptiness and shame that were experienced after an adulterous act, the despair and sorrow deeper still as shameful experiences in the sex industry are remembered. The heart grieves thinking how I was personally contributing to the pain and brokenness of a young prostitute that lay beneath me many times. These women were beautiful creatures of heart, full of potential but for some reason stuck as seemingly victims of circumstance and not knowing how to get out of a lifestyle, not wanting to, or simply can't. Every woman slept with in the sex industry was asked, "If God gave you a wish, what would it be?" Even though all of them were selling their bodies, not one of them wished for money or material possessions. These girls had old souls, much deeper and contemplative than the average Jane found on a city sidewalk. In tears of rivers and inner heart overflows I intently listened to their answers of my God question. As answers and heart conversations happened, they, too, had rivers of tears flowing as they looked back at the journey they called life.

One answered, "To know who I am." Amazed at this response, I intently looked at this beautiful girl now full of tears. How amazing and beautiful this heart. Holding her, I cried alongside her as she related her life story. Her mother is a prostitute and she was introduced into the sex industry by her sister at age 11! Hearing this, a weight of heavy shame came on me, and my tears bigger and life even more distressed as I peered deeper into this girl's heart and life and wondered how I could think of contributing to such brokenness in a magnitude impossible to even imagine. This was a dark moment. I was 47 years old, she 20. Another girl said, "I wish my mother did not abandon me as a child so that the five fathers in foster homes I lived in would not have raped me." I could not say anything to this, but felt my heart ripping, shredding in anguish, knowing my contribution to a further broken state. In tears, we cried together, holding each other. Two very broken individuals, hurting and not knowing how to get out of the shame we were head deep in. One girl did not know what to wish for, but instead exposes her heart and speaks of being raped at fourteen by a best friend's father while spending a night, and that all the wrong that is now happening with her was justified because she never said anything. What misguided understanding. This inflamed me, but who was I but just another contributor to her inner pain and brokenness. I am a father, my daughter being older than all the girls slept with in the sex industry. What a grievous shame, this ripped my heart further. It was no more the reflections of shameful acts that plagued my life and tore the heart apart but how do I get out of the shame and what to do about life going forward.

Of all the girls met in the sex industry, six close friendships developed, changed from casual encounters to meaningful ones. At invariable times of the day and night the girls would come and stay a few days, have long meaningful conversations of heart and we would always cry together and off they went. They would return with heads hung low, hurting, clearly from what they were doing with their bodies but did not know anything else much less a way out of a lifestyle that was the only thing any of them knew from a very young age. I was not fooling myself, we were all broken and in need of fixing and as much as I wanted to help fix them, broken will never fix broken. Knowing the difficulties in my own addictions, which at this point was not only drugs but sex and money, the task before any hurting and broken individual will not be easy, especially in confronting truth. To trust and believe in the beauty of Love never comes easy when everybody of significance, including ourselves, violates ideals we all hold dear in our hearts.

6

"Go and enjoy choice food and sweet drinks, and send some to those who have nothing prepared."

Nehemiah

The "boundary lines of joy" were rapidly falling. Never a time in life had so much liberty been felt. What crazy is this, that I was in a cold dungeon of steel, chained, and free from all that enslaved the heart, joyously partying without a narcotic substance in my body. And there before me were hundreds, if not thousands, of brothers stricken and paralyzed by fear while they waited for the disposition of the criminal cases against them. Feeling the most vibrant like no other time, faith was fueling a trust in the Lord who was intriguing and captivating, making me fall hard in love with Him. Feeling the hurting hearts of the many brothers, I wanted them to discover a liberation that was being felt. And as a surprise discovery of vocation,

the Lord inspired me to cook for the brothers and bring a message of hope. And thus, the "Ministry of Food" was borne in the house of steel.

My greatest prayer while detained was to be a good example of faith, hope, and love to all the hurting brothers. And to do this I first needed to tend to my heart, my grand commission. I was not going to provide a spiritual discourse of my life through some theoretical perspective of faith to my brothers who needed sometimes painful truth. My heart and faith were going to be expressed in how I lived and not through the words out of my mouth. And open doors to minister came as I simply concentrated on further knowing the Lord in a more richer way in my own life. The journey within affectively touched the world outside of me.

An all-out violent showdown was lurking for two days between principalities. Every dorm, balcony, and stairway had brothers staring each other down. For two days commanding officers ordered everyone to bunk status. While this was going on, I creatively began playing with an iced honey bun from the prison commissary and ended up making a rice pie with pudding and bananas that I chilled and shared. The pie must have tasted good, the brothers so easy to impress, because the next day after eating lunch 20 puddings and 9 bananas were found under my blanket. I smiled, looked to heaven, and knew exactly what the Lord wanted me to do about the brothers who were on the verge of war!

Enough pies were made to feed the warring factions. I had a few brothers clear two lockers of personal items, fill them with ice and chilled the pies. After an hour, I prayed, and went rounding up all the principality brothers: Blacks, Whites, Homies, Paisa's, English, Spanish, Spanglish, Americans, Mexicans and all the other -Cans and yes, even the -Cans that said they can't. The upper level of our dorm was packed, with commanding officer in our midst wondering to hit the panic button or not, trembling. Speaking to the brothers, myself nervous, they were told of the cooperation it took between the brothers to make all the pies, that the golden rule is to treat each other as we like to be treated, and that our differences did not make the world ugly but that much more beautiful. Closing my eyes, I raised my hands to heaven in surrender, and prayed for peace in all our hearts. Two lines were formed and I had the brothers pass out smiles, handshakes, and humble pie delicacies.

"Taking the five loaves and the two fish and looking up to

heaven, He gave thanks and broke them. Then He gave to the disciples to distribute to the people."

Dr. Luke

When the above bible verse in Luke 9 first came to life it was three months after entering the house of steel. Instead of five loaves of bread and two fish, however, it was an 8oz package of rice and a 4.23oz package of tuna, which amounted to something that more resembled a guppy or anchovy rather than a fish of any significant size. A single package of rice and tuna gives a four-inch piece of sushi roll to twenty brothers at a cost of 11.5 cents a person! A lot of ingenuity goes into making a sushi roll in a sterile prison environment. For example, my logical and analytical gifts provide an ability to see natural patterns and make empirical observations and conclusions. This is needed to determine how to make something sticky that is not (such as starchless rice) or to make pumpkin pie without pumpkin only a substance that smells like pumpkin but is not even edible! My forty plus years of mechanical experience is used to develop the tools needed to make a compressed sheet of rice that will not stick together. In a sterile environment of prison where there are no pieces of scrap metal laying around, hacksaws, saw-saws or cutting torches to fabricate or make holes in walls, only plastic sporks and bags, much ingenuity and mechanical aptitude is needed to make plastic into steel! My kinesthetic gift of good hand and "cross-eyed" coordination allows for three hands when four are needed but only have two! And finally, my aesthetic, creative appreciation provides an ability to create art out of bland ingredients to make delightful foods with only a wild imagination.

As a service of love, food as an opportunity was used to edify the many hurting brothers that were all around. This was not done as a favor for God but because it was a desire of the heart. I truly wanted the brothers to have and know the peace, joy, and security that were rapidly growing in my heart. I never set out to impress anyone, not a judicial judge, institutional staff member, not a brother, and definitely not God. My sole motivation was simply to know God and His will for my life, to live my heart out and not to win any favors from anyone, including a supernatural being. The grand commissioning, the journey, was inward, an inner understanding of Divine truth and validating this truth in the essence of my life and surroundings. And that truth was without a doubt Love!

How I came to a position of influence and favor among the thousands of brothers in the house of steel and the speed with which it happened, I do not know. I did not identify with a group, but had unlimited access to all the gangs, something that rarely happens. I loved all the brothers. The routine followed in the jail was not mainstream, different from all the rest. While everyone focused on joining gangs and finding security in the numbers or getting work details or joining drug programs for brownie points with the COs and the court, I focused on my heart. Although violence was very real in jail, I never got hurt. Many things were scary and harm could have easily come, but there was one thing for sure, I could not change who I am and was not about to try. No matter who the brothers were, it was their hearts that I was after, and all my sermons with the ministry of food were designed to edify each one of them whether directly or indirectly. The flock would always gather round during meal preparations and ask all kinds of questions, some personal, some irritating. And as a friendly reminder the brothers were always told that they were allowed one question a day and to use it wisely!

The Lord inspired my heart and hands using food with a purpose, and my whole heart was given, making sure love was in everything that was done. Recipes did not involve throwing a bunch of ingredients into a bowl, it involved inspiration, the wild imagination of all us brothers, and love to produce an unbeatable gourmet meal in a sterile prison environment with the craziest ingredients. The ministry of food exploded. Many miracles happened through the use of food, blessing, and transforming many areas of my heart and life. Many classic examples of Jesus feeding the five thousand happened.

During Sunday church service the chaplain would ask for prayer requests. While everyone asked for court hearings, lower prison sentences, and the usual boring requests, I would ask for new cooking recipes, and everyone, including the chaplain, would laugh. The way I saw it, it was against God's nature not to give everyone the very best. Therefore, why would not the Lord want all of us released from the house of steel--because it was to our detriment, we were not ready! I knew when our hearts were healed and restored we all would have a new song of life and the iron doors to the steel cage would open forever. The chaplain struggled with my unusual prayer request for new recipes, but joyfully brought it to the heart of the Lord. The following day during commissary, we find that all items that were usually available had all been changed three days before. All new ingredients meant new recipes. The Lord answered the unusual prayer request way before it was even asked. He knew! I was sure to mention the miracle to all at the following Sunday service. After announcing the miracle that happened the week before, the chaplain sternly asked, "Ibanez, any more unusual prayer requests?" I said, "Yes. Pray that we get our bananas back every Thursday." And sure enough, everyone hysterically laughed, again! Bananas were so universal for many eating delights. For three months, no bananas came with our Thursday morning meals. The chaplain playfully prayed for bananas, laughing all the way through, even forgetting what his sermon was about.

Wednesday arrived and bananas came with our morning meal, and it happened on Thursday as well! For the next three weeks, we had bananas twice a week! We were all amazed the first Wednesday morning, and brother after brother came high-fiving the whole day. Not only did we get our bananas back, but we got an extra day a week that came with bananas. A miracle indeed. The chaplain was now serious about my funny prayer requests, and about the faith in my heart that was by far bigger than a mustard seed.

It seemed that the power showing of the Lord would happen upon request, blessing the ministry of food that grew rapidly to the point of feeding a 100 plus brothers at a time, and planting seeds of hope in hearts using food. One morning while planning the making of many banana cheese cakes, I wanted pudding to garnish the cakes but had none. Thinking this in my heart, I looked to heaven. Lunch trays came and it was like "manna" from heaven appeared on the wilderness floor for the Israelites. On top of our lunch trays was pudding in three varieties of flavors. I cried. It was the Lord being super amazing! Another day, there were so many of us sick with the influenza virus on the floor. I dragged myself to eat, and there before me, vegetable soup, potato and cabbage salad, jelly, and peanut butter--a perfect meal for a bunch of sick people, that even gave all of us a smile. I cried, again, for the meal represented the smiling heart of the Lord.

The ministry of food was a powerful tool the Lord used to reveal Himself not only to me but to many brothers as well. Food with a purpose, to inspire hope, using love. Many brothers cried where they stood, in gratefulness for the love brought to their hearts using food. Many of them while on the outside had their last meal that was recycled from a trashcan. And now, out of the craziest ingredients found in a sterile prison environment, where a worn shoe and old sock were potential ingredients for a wild imagination and heart full of love, gourmet meals were being made.

Blood
&
Sweat

7

"For I neither received it of man, neither was I taught it, but by the revelation of Jesus Christ."

Paul of Tarsus

There are many times that the Divine must be seen and heard in a very real and tangible way, especially in times of trial and trouble when there is reliance on the self rather than trusting the Divine with the whole heart. A sign was not sought, for I already believed. Objective, empirical realities of God to follow, to direct, and to console were needed. Great books, including intelligent and charismatic people, were not going to be the venues that were going to teach about a Divine being and His nature. God was going to be the teacher, for man is going to fall too short of the mark. How can anybody resort to the feeble intellectual capabilities of man, genius or not, to

teach or know about an omniscient, omnipotent, and benevolent Being?

To know God has been the simple motivation of faith. Faith was not about making deals with God. Yes, I was in big trouble and very broken. Every law enforcement agency in the United States was in hot pursuit, the family, marriage, and friends were gone, professional career over, and in the dungeon of steel, chained, awaiting trial for felony drug conspiracy charges. God was not called upon for any of this. He was called upon to know, to show different than the broken and empty that it has always been.

Hundreds of churches have been attended, endless "how-to" programs tried, and the bible read at least three times in my lifetime, and nothing! Only when the motivations of my heart were pure did He reveal His nature, the richness of the bible come to life, and signs and wonders all over nature and everyday life that had a Divine signature began to intrigue, and imagination and fantasy went wild, and great inner joy filled the heart. Peace began to reign. Soon, everything became Divine acts of communication to validate faith and relationship with the Divine. Building structures began revealing prophetic messages. Peculiar events began happening. Natural laws were revealing absolute messages of a Divine being peculiarly involved in everyday minute details of life. Every little detail that revealed a fingerprint of the Lord proved to be a treasure of great joy. Tragedy, sorrow, and torment began to reveal truths of how beautiful and precious life is, every breath a gift. Looking toward an indescribable being that was captivating and intriguing, I saw past the pain and trouble and knew my heart was safe, my life directed and fully orchestrated. This was a gift to hear a voice so gentle and yet so powerfully great. The Lord, His nature, was proving to be very personal, leaving me wondering why few see or hear Him in a very real way.

As the intrigue began of how the Lord was revealing Himself, life took on a whole new flavor despite the many challenges that were being confronted in the steel dungeon. The "Jacob," the part of the self that runs around in religious activity when things go wrong, began to be seen in my own life and those of the many brothers in the house of steel. Jailhouse religion ran rampant. Church and bible study groups were filled with busy bodies on self-promotional campaigns showboating, to do favors on God's behalf in an effort for one in return, such as a lower prison sentence or a miracle get-out-of-jail-free card. Groups would grab bibles and study in front of the counselor's office and pray when COs were present. "Our Father" prayers and evangelizing being yelled all over, in corners and in the middle of rotundas, all with the premise of get-me-out-of-jail-God-because-I-am-helping-you-save-the-world!

Fasting and all kinds of mechanical/religious rituals and sacrifices were happening for the sole purpose of receiving some type of favor from God in exchange for a sacrifice. Wednesdays in the house of steel was always a favorite because many would give up their cheeseburgers as a religious fast of sacrifice. While all were thinking this ritual was going to win them brownie points with God, my belly would be filled to its cheeseburger delight! If only it were that easy; commit a crime, get caught, give up a weekly cheeseburger and then be let go! None of this was going to work. God did not want sacrifice from anybody. Isaiah 1:13 states, "Stop bringing meaningless offerings! Your incense is detestable to me." This verse is essentially saying sacrifice and sin offerings stink! In my heart, all self-promotional campaigns were meaningless and without substance so my motivations for calling on God were always deeply examined. The Lord wants me to honor His will, and His will is to love Him with my whole heart and not to give up my weekly cheeseburger! Being in love with the Lord, to show different from what has always been, was the desire and motivation, not because of being in jail but because I had an ugly, shameful, and meaningless existence.

Before and after being arrested I have sought to always be in alignment with the truth and to help another find their individual alignments. By intention, to deepen life. All experience carried a message, a truth to inscribe on the tablet of the heart. In a material world that tended to blind, the truth was sometimes hard to decipher. Therefore, motivation is key. If my motivation was not love out of a pure heart, then it was self-serving and selfish. Faith by example is how I want everybody to be affected. Any other way would be too hypocritical and there would be nothing concrete for anybody to touch. How I lived my life is the art and song that I wanted all to see, and it better be Love as an active and wholehearted expression.

Making the voice of the Lord real for the many brothers who were searching for different was the goal, to have them latch on to what was driving me with great joy. To have them see what was being seen all over, something real and personal that was allowing to see beyond failure, mistakes, uncertainty, and pains of a previous existence that chased the urges of the flesh. The brothers knew that there was a confidence that I was trusting with the whole heart. Love is the confidence, that made me still, while the many ran around in different directions in desperation, in fruitless self-efforts to try and open prison doors when the real locks that needed to be opened were the ones that held their hearts captive.

And how clever is God who knew all our ways and not only creates the possibilities to which we can be blocked but also provides a clearing for His voice of Love to be heard, for a new foundation to be built, and for a new song in life to be sung. This was the message that spoke forth from every surrounding wall in the fortified contemporary dungeon of the steel cage. God speaking, longing to embrace our hearts as He watches us on the fence of life, and not pushing us over but tenderly courts us to His side.

To go big, be the best, achieve the most, and take everything to the extreme, even the poison that went into my body, are personal attributes always known for. With passion and heart all was done, and this was no different with faith. Perfection was sought. Not perfection in regards to my fallible nature but in knowing truth and its consistent application in all life circumstances, the good and the bad. Life is taken very seriously. No games were being played with God, my heart, or any of the brothers in the house of steel. Nobody. Faith is very personal and is not about glory show-boating of the self. There is nothing to boast of. A lifelong struggle with drugs brought pain and hurt to many lives. And in some cases, death. Hearts are taken seriously, and I wanted the many hurting brothers to have what was being lived, freedom. Freedom from fear, failure, helplessness, hopelessness, and slavery to pain, hurt, and evil desires of the flesh. No other way was known other than to have an authentic faith and live out the example in sincere love for my brothers. Hearts were not stirred with fancy lip service but by a real life and a real example, to see before their eyes and touch the product of sincere and wholehearted faith--true hope.

Many walked the corridors of steel as if they had no hope. The pain and fear in eyes can clearly be seen, desperate hearts transparent and visible. They reach and grab at anything they think would give them some sense of control, but nothing works and families and relationships falter even further, and the ramifications of their mistakes paralyzed them with fear as 10- and 20-year prison sentences hang over their heads.

The brothers had troubles, and I, too, had similar if not bigger troubles than most of them. Fatherhood, marriage, friendship, family, and career were all gone, and a twenty-year prison sentence was hanging over my head. The United States Justice department was pounding hard at my door, thoroughly examining everything. Their scrutiny has been unrelenting. The day my marriage ended, I flew in from Chicago O'Hare and landed in San Diego, California, and life has never been the same since. This was December 27, 2011, the day Homeland Security Immigration Custom Enforcement (ICE) made their presence known outside the airport terminal on the city sidewalk asking to search my bags for drugs and money. From here, they were everywhere. At the post office, postal inspectors escorted me to back offices for questioning, requesting all mail pieces and parcels be opened before them. Shopping in a supermarket, they were there. On public transportation going to church, they were there. On the phone and world wide web, they were there. At home, around the clock they were there. In jail, they were there. Everywhere, Blue-Shoes were there. And today, they are still here, kicking stuff around and turning rocks over!

Many arrows have flown by none other than the dirty devil himself, wanting me to hate everybody, all those who hurt and pursue with evil intent. Every arrow has faltered and fell to the ground. And nobody has been hated. All of them have been given front row seats to my faith, heart, and life, to see my pain and suffering, challenges and triumphs, as a source of encouragement and edification, to see and touch hope. Everything has proven to be beautiful no matter the season, whether on mountain tops or the valley lows, victories, or painful defeats, because through it all the Lord has revealed Himself. This is the treasure and the joy, Love! Nothing mattered, not the United States of America verses Christopher Ibanez nor the pain and hurt in the heart but hearing the voice of the Lord however He chose to speak.

In the past, church life and faith amounted to a mechanical routine with very little substance. If supernatural occurrences were happening, none were recognized. Intellectually, I knew who God was--a Divine being somewhere "out there." Faith, however, had no substance and produced nothing for life. Higher education produced a successful career with many accomplishments but an emptiness was always felt and grew deeper with time and achievement. It was not until much later in life that the Lord was recognized as being very personal when He blocked a suicide attempt one morning when He caused a video message from my daughter and granddaughter to come a millisecond before death entered my veins. In a desperate moment, the Lord touched my heart and forever changed the direction of life with a gentle voice and warm embrace that comforted in a raging storm of life.

Before God, every heart is revealed. And so, my heart was always examined and daily emptied of all that weighed it. The last four years has been a fire, burning and purifying the fields of the heart, and in the fertile ground of ash the beauty of freedom is borne, love causing life to blossom. It mattered not that I was caged in the house of steel, for freedom is not a place but a reality. Because the heart is free from the prisons of idolatry that once held it captive, the beauty of life abounds. In the house of steel, that is supposed to be jail and affliction, there was a freedom that was never known before. The heart and mind were seeing clearly and waiting on the Lord to reveal His glory was the only thing longed for. There have been so many miracles in the past four years that it is hard to shut-up about any of it.

Why so late in life God has come to be known in a personal way is a wonder. He is a beauty that keeps on being discovered in an adventure, where around every bend a new revelation is discovered of the Lord's omniscience and omnipotence. Every surprise is a profound joy that fills me with awe and love, to pass on and affect someone with. A simple extension, expression or even a gesture of love touches the heart of anyone. Brothers, with tear-filled eyes, would say I am different and real, by a simple expression of love. The difference is that the face of Jesus has been touched and His love experienced through His body, my brothers who were clearly hurting and were sincerely served. With a little contemplation and reflection, they will find that there are no other explanations, no other truth in this world, that explains a heart given in love to all, in sincere servitude and hospitality to all individual needs.

Even with all the challenges confronted in the dungeon of steel, all has been amazingly beautiful. The journey through the furnace has filled the heart with an indescribable substance. To share and build memories and experiences of life is very personal. Lives have been transformed, this overwhelms. The deepest hurt and fears of the brothers have been shared, this overwhelms. The brothers have shared my heart with their families, this overwhelms. Together with their families, we have visited, laughed, and cried together, and this overwhelms. Been given a privilege to see and know the depth of individual brokenness and darkest corners of hearts and highest aspirations in life, and this overwhelms. And have helped in the building of different visions and dreams of many brothers, and this overwhelms, honorably humbles me. All of them have been loved as deep as possible, unconditionally, in sincerity and truth. This is all special and fills the heart with a beauty beyond measure.

Many that I have met in the house of steel want freedom, but most do not even know what freedom is. Many think it is through the locks of the iron cage or even at the expense of another. Being free to walk the streets of the world does not signify freedom from the many things that hold us captive and slaves to the very lifestyles that landed us in jail. Prison, whether in the dark confines of a jail cell or in homes of elite neighborhoods, is the condition of the heart. There are many that walk in wayward and lost circles everywhere. The vicious cycling is a revolving door, with brothers cycling two, three, four times through correctional institutions. Recidivism rates are reported as 60%. It is more like 90%! I do not need elaborate statistical processing methods to give probable values when before my eyes I see the hard numbers.

Clearly it was sensed that some brothers

wanted different, but did not know how to achieve it, asking everybody except the Lord. This, I thought was the craziest idea. Everybody wants to know about the Lord but they do not bother to ask *Him*. I find it ironic that a Divine being with which they seek, one that is all-knowing, and all-good, they try to know through people, doctrines of the world, sound programming, and great literature and intelligent minds in past and present times, rather than the Divine Spirit. Everybody has always been told that God, Lord Jesus, is not known by what I have read in any book, nor by what anybody has told me, including pastors, but by seeking the Spirit out with the whole heart. How can anybody pass the source of knowledge and settle for the mediocre substance of man to know the essence of Love? No one can be deceived by anyone if the source of communication is Divine. When the Lord speaks to someone personally, that individual will know without a doubt and will be forever changed.

911
2522
2412

8

"The heavens declare the glory of God; the skies proclaim the work of His hands. Day after day they display knowledge. There is no speech or language where their voice is not heard. Their voice goes out into all the earth, their words to the ends of the world."

King David

Throughout my Christian journey, I wanted Jesus to be a real substance and experience. My mind is objective and empirical, always scientific. In the cold house of steel many unusual and peculiar events began happening, events that were impossible to be coincidental or accidental chance occurrences. It was without a doubt Divine communication. This grounded me, strengthened my faith, deepened my joy, and invigorated my hope in the valley of uncertainty.

God is absolute, and therefore should communicate through absolute means. This was the

reasoning when a 9:11 numeric pattern was discovered, and every new discovery was captivating, leaving me in awe. My house number and that of a best friend Peanuts, the most influential person to my faith, are 2412(9) and 2522(11). Individually, these numbers sum to 9:11. The physical address of the federal detention center that held me is 808 Union Street, San Diego, CA, 91201 and that of the federal court that would oversee the criminal case against me is 221 West Broadway San Diego, CA, 91201. Individually summed, the numbers in these addresses come to 9:11. All these places were not areas that were chosen, at least not intentionally as it relates to being arrested--I did not choose to be arrested and housed in a steel cage!

This was only the beginning, a foreshadow of things to come, for the 9:11 pattern plagued my life I would soon find. It was very peculiar and intriguing. What did it mean? The pattern started appearing as life and circumstantial events began being reflected upon. The one sure thing that was known, that the 9:11 pattern was not a chance occurrence or event of coincidence. It was the Lord, saying, "I, the Lord God, knew all the time." This was liberating!

After a year in custody, I was somehow signed

up to meet with a psychologist for a monthly couch session of Freudian "free association." On my first visit, the doctor was told that voices are not heard but seen. And like all typical psychologists who hear a "crazy" statement like this, the doctor jumped right on to the bait like a fish on a hook and asked to explain this "seeing voices." She was told about the 9:11 numeric pattern that kept showing up in significant and peculiar times and about messages that were being revealed in architecture and structures. I named off a slew of examples and she said, "That's interesting." I said, "No, it is God!" It was God, and He was and is Divinely communicating to everyone who is willing to listen.

Intrigued and captivated, numbers were closely examined. Nine is the number of the Spirit, and 90 when summed as individual numbers equals 9 (i.e. 9+0=9). Every architectural endeavor ever accomplished has its foundation on the 90-degree geometric principle. God inspired this. In building structures, it can be seen below design and feature and into the principle workings and absolute truth that enable anything to be built, the 90-degree right angle. No matter what was looked at, the right angle was speaking a voice. On a tiled floor are crosses everywhere. On a wall, a door, a window, everything had a cross. A new world had been opened. Everywhere the fingerprints of God were being seen. Everywhere one looks, there are crosses. From the outer reaches of the cosmos in the form of stars to the smallest molecular structures of life called laminin are crosses, the voice of Jesus saying "I love you" every step taken and sight looked upon.

Every city in the world has a message waiting to be discovered, a Divine treasure implanted by God through the hands of unknowing builders so all anyone has to do is open their heart and accept the gift of His Spirit and the Lord will open their eyes and reveal the treasure of His beautiful heart for them. The San Diego Convention Center, the widest and longest building in the city, is shaped as a giant arrow. The arrow points to a giant three-dimensional cross that is the Marriot South Tower that is not a hundred feet away! How crazy is this, that God Divinely making the structures unknowingly built and placed in such a way to communicate a message and Jesus saying here is My cross, My love for all, for life, free and beautiful. These messages implanted in building structures and architectural design are not random and accidental or even incidental events or occurrences. They are very intentional in purpose, strategically placed, with a Divine source that is undeniably communicating.

Figure 2: This is an aerial view of the San Diego Convention Center and Marriot South tower. Examining building shapes, the convention center is an arrow that points to an outward protruding cross not 1000 feet away that is the Marriot tower.

When Divine details were discovered in my life, that were implanted years past and extending sometimes through generations, I got a real impression of how vastly involved God is with life, meaningfully attentive in the littlest details. Every step of the way there has been some type of Divine communication happening. These events are peculiar and intriguing. There was no more the possibility of chance or coincidence that an unusual event happened, but rather what did it mean and what was the message the Lord intended me to understand and apply to my heart. The 9:11 numeric pattern was constantly happening at strategic times, as if being directional

signs to follow. And scripture in my devotional readings and at the bottom of my journal pages were aligning with the stirrings of my heart at peculiar times, speaking forth a message that would minister for exactly what I was going through. This is profound, for as I thought about how far in time the Lord knew when something would be needed, this intrigued me how He put it in place so far into the past. This was mind blowing! Everything was set in place, weaved through the fabric of time.

"How precious also are Your thoughts to me, O God! How vast is the sum of them!"

King David

Every morning the brothers would collect raisins from their cereal and give me these versatile commodities for cooking. When the collection would come, the raisins were counted, sometimes up to three times just to confirm the number, and the totals would always sum to 9 or 11(i.e. 9, 27, 83, 36, 90, 164, etc.)! This happened every time we were served raisin bran cereal in the morning, and every time this gave great joy.

Although 9:11 were predominately the numbers used to communicate a message, other numbers were used as well, making everything even more intriguing. During Sunday church service, the chaplain was asked to pray for the number 10. After giving a funny look and some laughter about my unusual request, he asked what about the number. I told him Jesus knows, just to pray for the number 10! The number 10 signifies a Divine cycle completion, which at the time there were tremendous struggles with Blue-Shoes operatives attacking on many fronts, trying to get a jailhouse confession that would link me to a criminal network. This was challenging and I wanted this cycle in the case to be over and that was why the chaplain was asked to pray for the number 10. After the chaplain prayed, he did not give a sermon but instead played a movie about laminin, which looked like a cross when viewed from an electron microscope. Laminin is the smallest particle of DNA that tells chromosomes what and when to do something in the formation of life. The narrator of the movie states that it takes two sets of chromosomes, 23 plus 23, to make a person. What caught my attention was these numbers summed to 10(2+3+2+3)! This spoke two things that answered my prayer for the number 10, an answer that was given before I even asked for it! First, the cross between the two sets of chromosomes signifies I am made in the image of Christ. Second, because I am made in His image I must love because Christ is love. This meant that my Blue-Shoes brothers were no different than I and therefore they had to be loved whether I liked it or not.

Numbers were a big way Divine messages were conveyed, but what was more intriguing and revelatory were dreams and how the Lord uses them to speak a personal message to the dreamer. How I came to interpret dreams I am not sure, only that when dreams were related images came to mind and I simply spoke from the heart and a story emerged. The messages were very specific and provided clues that pointed to issues that were weighing the heart. Dreams, in my opinion, are some of the most prophetic messaging venues used for individual edification and journey. There were many times brothers would come with troubling issues that we had a hard time putting a finger on, like what they wanted to tell a judge during sentencing or trying to gain understanding on a deteriorating marriage where there are never any easy answers or sure solutions. I would tell the brothers to sleep on it and an answer would come to heart, and sure enough the individual would have a dream with a message. Their eagerness and promptness to come back for a dream interpretation is clear evidence that they had recognized that some type of miracle had happened while they slept. Soon, brothers were coming asking about their dreams, and I simply spoke from my heart and what was seen. Brothers would cry, would ask how particular details were known, and would run off telling others about intriguing dream interpretations. Some brothers even came asking for their fortunes to be told as if I was some fortune teller with a crystal ball. I laughed.

9

"Let our curiosity, adventure, and wonder of life never end. Those that expose themselves as knowing the truth, lose the battle of innocence and humility and eventually pull a trigger at the universe. Wisdom chooses the unknown to be its reason."

Akiane Kramarik[iii]

Many unusual circumstances started happening, circumstances that had no explainable source other than a Divine one. Anybody can manipulate circumstances to deceive, but when nobody else knows anything about events except the person involved there is an undeniable certainty of the experience and the truth. My heart played no games. My mind, always objective and empirical. This was God speaking, the source behind the unusual events, Divinely communicating through many venues, providing revelation and testimony of Him during very troubling times. I simply followed His voice that called,

that led me to trust. Trusting and believing that life and all the crazy that was happening would get better seemed impossible. Family and marriage gone, career over, arrested in one of the largest criminal conspiracy cases in southern California, and chained in the house of steel, it seemed all was getting worse.

In the house of steel, the 9:11 numeric pattern was showing up all over the place, the ministry of food was powerfully at work and enormously growing, the edification of many hurting brothers could not be contained, and many miraculous wonders were transforming and propelling me forward. All these were considered Divine food, the "Manna" from heaven while in the desert, the Metropolitan Correction Center in downtown San Diego. My life had been shaken, and I was having an amazing time at a minimum.

My life flourished, renewed so powerfully. As the Lord's voice grew clearer, life became sacred. Eating with the brothers, breaking bread in the form of cooking and sharing food and my life with them, communing together in our challenges of everyday life in jail, and shared fellowship of pain and hurt, failure and dreams, all had become sacred. Soon, the dungeon of steel became the kingdom of heaven. I was free.

No deals were being made with God, nor were there ever any prayers to get out of the steel cage. A different song of life was desired, and different did not require getting out of jail. And unfailing, the Lord always found some peculiar way to Divinely communicate and this always had me leaping for joy. Intriguing, too, was how He was heard all around, Divine encounters of circumstance through people, nature, and even food. Visions in my sleep had me awaking knowing how to make pizza with ramen noodle soup, stale bread, and cheese that beat the pizza served by the institution. The brothers loved the Divinely touched food that was made. It was amazing how this was all happening. Jesus "fed the five thousand" many times. Not with two fish and five loafs of bread but with a banana and two sleeves of saltine crackers! All of us were being transformed, touched in the craziest way by a very peculiar God using food!

One day while cleaning tables after the dinner serving, I was rushed into our range by a brother named "Tarzan" who literally was trying to pull me through the iron bar doors. Tarzan was insistent that I come in and held me until the commanding officer came to open the door, and I wondered why this brother desperately needed me. In jail, this usually signifies a beat down was going to happen. When I got in the range, there was a giant table made of lockers, piled high with nachos to feed a million brothers, and all the brothers gathered around. As I descended the stairs, the "Paisa" principality leader said, "Chris, for you, for love, from all of us, thank you." This was overwhelming. What did I do to deserve this? With eyes full of tears, the brothers were told that everything is done with the whole heart and it is an honor and privilege to serve all of them in love. I was blown away by how profoundly Jesus used my life without me even knowing it. These brothers, “Mi Familia,” I will never forget, for they played a vital role in teaching about love and the profound meaning, pleasure, and treasures of servitude.

Many times, I woke early to find my only alone time with the Lord in a dorm of 200 plus brothers. As I listened to worship music, reflecting on life, I come to realize that we, all of us people, are brothers and sisters in this world full of struggle and strife. We are family. I gaze upon my sleeping brothers on double bunks up against every wall and available space. I think about all of them and their families that are seen during visitation times and my heart swells knowing the full weight of how they have positively affected me, becoming a very personal part of my heart, that will forever be honored and reflected upon for the lessons of love they have all taught me. But I also grieve for them and their families. They are all hurting, scared, and wondering the disposition of their lives as it has been affected by their mistakes. I have always helped them focus on their hearts, the inner journey within and who they are because that is where the problem lies and not on the mistake.

Life is giant. My footprints on the roads traveled were made to make everything as meaningful as possible by ensuring my whole heart has been in all, authentically applied. Even amidst challenge and misfortune, being true to my heart meant that I would not live in regret. It also challenged me to flesh out life in every moment to not take life for granted. Discovering my meaning and connection to all the world, my song, and a God that intrigues through subtle ways of communicating has always been the content of my reflections. God sometimes takes everything to the edge of understanding, requiring a leap of faith and a release of the self and understanding to trust and believe that it is the Lord who is ever-present and always working.

The answer to everything, my pain, hurt, and challenges, the longings of my heart, and my future is love. Many things have been chased in this world and I have only found pain and disappointment at the end of the road. Love, however, is much bigger than who we are and is the key that opens a door to a life different than it has always been. Love is beautiful. It is open and free. Love instructs and gives confidence, allows sight to see life in its richness and beauty. I look back at life and see all that has happened, all that has been experienced, all trials and tremendous struggles that piled challenge after challenge, all the sources of pain and hurt, and I can still say life is beautiful, beautiful because sin does not complicate it anymore. Being thrown in the dungeon of concrete and cold steel meant that I was not arrested, nor jailed, but rescued! One day, as the iron barred window of the steel cage was looked out of, my million-dollar beach front view in downtown San Diego, I asked myself how life would improve if I were to be let out that very second. The answer was surprising, for there was not a worry in the world. Of course, I wanted out of the steel cage like everyone else, but I was already free, freed from a world that held me captive and slave to all the wrong ideals in life.

PAIN
SHAME
GUILT
FEAR
BONDAGE
DEATH

10

"I praise you, Father, Lord of heaven and earth, because you have hidden these things from the wise and learned, and revealed them to little children."

Jesus of Nazareth

A brother once said, "We have been the continued expressions of life as those adults who influenced us--fathers, mothers, uncles, gangsters." What an intriguing statement. We are a continued cycle of those before us who somehow influenced us. They affected us, captured our imaginations, and have shielded the true identities of who we are in our hearts. Vicariously, we have become people who we are not, off chasing the ideals of those before us and come to the same ends, empty, broken, living dysfunctional lives, and being detached from our meaning and purpose, grossly misaligned vocationally. What a destiny of irony, a lifecycle never broken out of, two, three, four generations on either direction of the dimension of time. How sad, scary, and horribly crazy. Everywhere I look, people merely existing, settling in circumstance, accepting that life is superficial rather than meaningful and full. All human effort covering individual lifespans is spent fruitlessly trying to achieve the so-called "American dream" of another rather than something far richer in substance, Love.

On the rooftop of the fortified steel dungeon I sat watching and wondering of the thousands of brothers with lost hearts searching for answers in a life they have no clue what is about, without even a hint of their individual gifts or vocation. Virtually all of them show the different symptoms of the same problem, a wayward heart caught in the swirl of a meaningless and crazy existence that opens the same doors of emptiness and despair repeatedly. There are clearly different categories of brothers. There are the simple innocent ones, which are preyed upon and used and abused in this dog eat dog world of greed, recruited by drug cartels to serve unknowingly as scapegoats in the grandeur scheme of criminal enterprise. There are those who half know what is going on and jump into a life of crime head first seeing only dollar signs but do not have a clue how to get around and find themselves in a pit wondering which way is out and refuse to look up. And finally, there are those who are very intelligent, the leaders of the principalities and their affiliates. The intelligent ones I have wondered about many times. These guys stand above the rest and make all the decisions for their individual parties, and many times selfishly prey upon the flock in which they lead. They are searching for a life that they are missing, but chase their tails because they refuse to let go of the lifestyle they have chosen to stay in. These guys fully know that everything about their lives is pulling them further away from who they are. Life, love, family, and individual vocations are in great misalignment with the lifestyles chosen. Rather than reevaluate what is happening they scramble to make everything fit, to put square pegs in circles and blame everybody but themselves why nothing is working right. And then, to add insult to injury, they settle with being self-appointed victims of circumstance. And church and spiritual authority offer no answers and are just as misaligned as everything else that is before their eyes. They find the climb out of the pit is increasingly fruitless as they watch their lives spiral faster down into the abyss of emptiness, regret, and lost opportunity as natural life rapidly disappears. They see the imposing walls of the steel cage as a restriction rather than an opportunity and a powerful source of freedom, that carry a voice that says the real prison is the ideals of the heart that enslave individual life conditions.

"A bird doesn't sing because it has an answer, it sings because it has a song."

Maya Angelou[iv]

Circumstances happen in life, with no identifiable reasons sometimes, leaving many questions rather than any sure answers. In the struggle to understand, to find answers, we are left in wonder and reach for reason and find excuse for lost opportunity to live the individual, unique song of who we are. We then grow further apart from the heart and thereby are conformed to outer forces and influences rather than shapers of individual destiny. Each of our lives are different and very individual, a unique song of beauty, a melody of love in a life full of valleys and heights to negotiate and appreciate opportunity to live and cherish every moment of life. Instead of singing the song of our lives through individual evolution of vocation, we get caught up searching for answers and reasons for the whys, find excuse, and then go off chasing everything that is not who we are—money, possessions, status and dreams of another. Then, live in regret. And finally, die! How sad that so many beautiful lives end this way, that when death comes to the door, life is taken rather than given to the other side because it was not free and full of meaning, fulfilled through love.

"Influence Magazine" published an article by Mark Batterson titled, "*Writing Your History*." The following is very revealing and disheartening, but very relevant to how we as people get tragically lost in the journey of life and become conformed by the world rather than having footprints that influenced the shaping of life through individual uniqueness. Mark states, "At some point, most of us stop living out of imagination and start living out of memory. That's the day we stop creating the future and start repeating the past. That's the day we stop living by faith and start living by logic. That's the day we stop dreaming of what if possibilities and end up with if only regrets." And finally, Mark lists the "Top Five Regrets of the Dying," with the number one being, "I wish I'd had the courage to live life true to myself, not the life others expected of me."[v]

This is a sad truth that many in life will find as a reality. Life is much more than an existence of nutrition and mental stimulation or behavioral preoccupation. An insect or even a worn shoe has a more profound existence than this. Too often we live superficial and shallow lives and find ourselves empty, vocationally misaligned, and addicted to anything to try and fill a void because we are so far removed from who we are, almost completely withdrawn because life has no substance, no meaning and fulfillment. We go off chasing that which looks good, that entice us. Money, power, beautiful women, professional careers, and material possessions are the portraits of common wisdom and contemporary thought that say "life." Dreams and individual visions are vicarious, stolen art that belongs to another, not our own unique works of individual substance drawn from the essence of who we are and called to be.

From church pews and podiums to the highest levels of government and organizational hierarchies in corporate business to low class and high class and to the poor and filthy rich, we find dysfunctional families, relationships, and individuals. We find people wondering what life is about and for what meaningless reason empty promise has been passionately pursued, coming home with unfulfilled hearts and illusive rest. When sleep is found, a new day rises only to repeat the nightmare of the day before. This is not only scary, it is sad and disturbing because across the world there is death, violence, suicide, addiction, crime, and every crazy thing under the sun that happens because we fail to see just how profoundly beautiful we are and the life we have been given, missed in the midst of the enticing voices of the world and selfish-me minds looking for recognition and validation in all the wrong places. Everything becomes a boast, a look at me and what I have accomplished, my million dollars and mansion in the sky. After the empty recognitions and plaques, silence in the home finds restlessness, emptiness and despair, and self-inflicted wounds to the head from gunshots that splatter brains on the walls in which the plaques of empty recognition hang. What a sad destiny of irony. Then, adding insult to injury, the vicious cycle repeats in the next generation, and the next, and the next.

The one sure thing that I saw with many brothers in the house of steel was that many were being actors in the movie of life, carrying and living stolen art rather than being artists drawing their individual portraits on the landscape of existence. This is what got them into trouble and kept them searching for an elusive meaning in the chase for wealth through ill-gotten means. Rather than discovering who they are in the opportunity of jail, and identifying their individual and unique gifts and vocations, time is spent occupying the mind and not examining the inner workings of the heart. And the unlocking of steel doors is just a different day, with no real change of the heart. If change has happened, then mistakes become educational opportunities that help develop and strengthen individual hearts. Unfortunately, for the majority, the cycling and revolving doors of prison spin out of control. This may be a hidden blessing, a call to awaken to different, for if not the locking door of a jail cell it could very well be the sealing nails of a box of rest in peace!

The federal judicial system does no justice by giving reduced sentences to offenders that cooperate and work both sides of the law, for the inevitable is only prolonged. The system rewards the "snitch" program, and many brothers run to this false sense of security and therefore never become free from the prisons of their hearts, even though they may just get released much earlier than expected. Freedom is not through prison doors that lead to the outside world. It is the inner world of the heart that has identified a uniqueness, an individual beauty, that trusts the voice of love to transform and purify, to borne new dreams and discover life in a world filled with infinite possibilities. This is freedom, freedom to know who we are in the discovery of life and love. It is not enough to wake and tread the earth without purpose. A worn shoe has a more profound meaning. Every step must see a different reality, and everything touched should forever affect and be transformed themselves. Whatever this connection may be, or shall however happen is no matter, it is the meaning and depth with which the heart has been applied, for it is a personal extension and expression of love. Time passes too fast to forego an elevated opportunity to positively affect another forever. Every day the boundaries of the grave widen, and it does not want to be entered with regrets because the earth was roamed living in the mind rather than completely subdued with the whole heart.

A little reflection reveals truth in which we walk. Is it who we are, even amidst mishap and serious blunder, or is it stolen art being acted out in the landscape of life lost in. Too much emphasis is put on mainstream portraits of others to reflect identity, that profess life that is not who we are or even close to the life wanted. Wealth and materialism and their values drive modern day thought, and this is the stolen art that actors live rather than being artists, directing the unfolding 3-D movie of individual flavor and personality. Dreams of materialism and wealth must change to the beauty with which all are individually created. Until this change happens, the same dead-end song of our minds will be the product of life that is so

far out of tune with who we are.

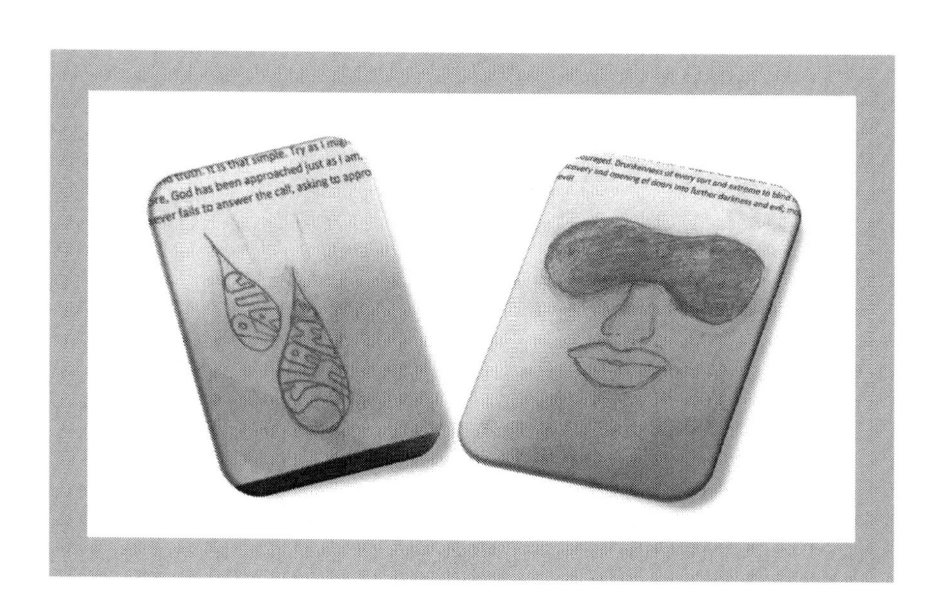
truth. It is that simple. Try as I
God has been approached just as I am,
fails to answer the call, asking to
Drunkenness of every sort and extreme to blind
and opening of doors into further darkness and evil,

11

"In the midst of his plenty, distress will overtake him; the full force of misery will come upon him."

Job

There are many voices in the world that falsely show us in a very real and concrete way the direction to go. Inconspicuous influences of people, culture and traditional schools of thought tend to drive our aspirations that are not uniquely individual. These ideals come in many forms and can be very complex and dynamic in the human heart. Looking back in my life it becomes clear how culture and tradition influenced the "vision and dream" of what life should be, that life and meaning meant being successful materialistically and financially. All effort was spent surrounding these ideals.

The meaningless race for more, more of everything, brought my life down. More drugs, more

girls, and more money equated to chaos and crazy, the building of an empire of shame that piled high the sins of the heart. The land of plenty, plenty of pain, broken lives, and troubles with the law. Reflections in the house of steel had me one day pondering the idea of more. Everybody had plenty of something, and yet we find ourselves wanting more than end up feeling even more emptier than before we had anything! The irony of more in the land of plenty! In my land of plenty, plenty of sex and poison in the veins, all was broken. No matter what horizon gazed upon--marriage, family, career--there was only distress and despair, and a desire for more poison in the veins to numb a broken reality. The needle was always full of poison, filling the veins, and flirting with death at every pop of a vein with the needle of a syringe to escape the filth of sin. Then, piercing arrows would come from all directions--family, friends, and enemies. And with hate and penetrating words, fire was breathed back before crawling back into the cave of filth. No matter what came, there was powerful reason and rational as a double barrel shotgun with bullets that would blast any life that dare challenge. Arguments were strong and means did not matter so long as the ends were achieved--hate and hurt! The life, broken. The poison in the veins, victimless. How wrong. The family was hurting deeply, and the destruction of lives caused by the drugs that I helped put into the streets of world destinations amounted to countless victims and destroyed lives.

In the confines of prison walls, it was easy to read the body expressions of the many brothers. Fear gripped and paralyzed many of them. A life anchored in worldly ideals has finally caught up to them, and mistakes and failures has drowned life out to an existence that even the simplest life forms have more meaning. Families torn apart, significant relationships are held together with fractured threads, and the brothers desperately reach for anything to stay in control of a world that the bottom has fallen out of. They think the song of life is different because the day has changed, but to family members it is even more clearer, nothing has changed other than a locked steel door. Family members are torn further apart, for they love those connected to them but they want different from the same song of life that has become so dead out of tune. Abuse, pain, hurt, and dysfunction has now cycled across generational gaps and speaks a voice that tells them there is no hope for a different tomorrow.

On the inside, many brother's re-live mistakes,

further paralyzing their lives. They stare at the ceiling with fear-stricken eyes, drag their heads on the ground, all living in the past or at some time in the future to be someone rather than realizing that now is the ordained time to prune and circumcise the heart so that the true prison doors are forever opened, to know who they are meant to be and the future life that they are to live. This begins in present moments, not yesterday's failures or tomorrow's opportunities. Today everything begins. Being sober starts now. They fail to see this because they are trapped in yesterday's mishaps rather than harvesting the excellent opportunities Divinely given now to see, to see just how beautiful they are. Mistakes are ugly, but life is beautiful and they must see it as such. The blinders to seeing the beautiful life before them are from the feeble ideals of their hearts, the driving force behind every wayward and prodigal person. This world offers us table scraps, and in our greed, we commit crimes and prostitute our hearts for more!

The whole federal judicial system is about greed. The drug cartels, the defense lawyers, and virtually every detainee in jail, are all driven by greed. Currently, the influx of arrests into the federal judiciary system is costing billions of dollars annually. The drug cartels want money and will use anybody or anything to get it. The lawyers sharing the billions of dollars to defend clients make easy greed money. And every federal crime committed by all of us in the federal system is related to money. Widening the picture, money, in the world's eyes, means better. Virtually everyone is driven to get more money, more of everything. The "American dream" was a wonderful ideal, but now only represents the letter in which it was written and not the spirit in which it was borne, essentially bastardizing the ideal! This is why the influx of drugs into America will not end but only increase. The problem is not the Mexican drug cartels and their affiliations that work the American-Mexican border and the drug dealers that riddle the American landscape and have faces of mothers, fathers, and children. It is hearts that are full of wrong ideals, chasing dreams that are not personal and uniquely individual but is stolen art from mainstream philosophy of capitalist driven people. Lifetimes are spent chasing wealth, only to come home in silence and still find that something is missing even with everything before us--family, wealth, power, and possessions. From here, despair and regret set in and an escape from reality is sought. Soon, it's run, run, run. Run to the bars for margaritas. Run to social media and brag about happiness and joy that is not there. Run to sex, drugs, and shame. Run from silence to avoid the picture of our lives that is given.

Violence was always present in the house of steel. What was more troubling was the greed that ran rampant in many hearts throughout the jail. Greed is what caused many violent showdowns among the brothers. All around there was greed beyond measure, driving the brother's hearts and lives further into the dark abyss. What was the Lord saying about greed, I remember thinking? The Lord says to give unconditionally. There were so many around that had need, so many having their meals stolen, greed trampling upon everything. Why should I give or care for any of the greedy ones, I thought? Then the Lord spoke, saying, He takes from the poor to give to the rich. The humble in heart give even what little they have materially and give abundantly of themselves in love. This stirs the hearts of the greedy, for there is greater treasure in giving then there is in taking.

One morning the kitchen orderlies were ready to bust each other's heads open for food. Each were grabbing whatever they wanted and argue because one got more than the other. And then, the ranges come out to eat and there is not enough food to feed all the brothers. Day in and out this is watched and I struggle with myself. Shutting my mouth is the hardest thing, but I also know that no amount of words or beatings will change these brothers from scavenging everything in sight. First, they sold drugs to land in jail and now they cheapen themselves by peddling cockroaches. Anything they can find will be sold, even a dirty underwear, which they will insist and tirelessly say it is a good deal at a fair price! As my anger builds, I am reminded, even convicted, that I too at one time sold my soul just to get a fix of poison in my veins, a thrill in my pants, and a dollar in my pocket, going to the extremes to stack George Washington's and Thomas Jefferson's in piles and destroying lives in the process. The gods of wealth had driven me into a pit, salivating in sin, and having orgies with the devil.

More of everything for a false sense of security. From soap, food, toothpaste, and possessing every available brand of shoes sold at the prison commissary. These are all signs of greed. Whether its hoarding the yucky bran flakes cereal that is served for breakfast or the billions of dollars it is costing the federal government to prosecute drug offenses, it is all greed.

The "Great Silence" is a place of revelation, where opportunity abounds. The voices of the world pull in many directions, to confuse. Professional careers demanding a better bottom line, worries that linger and carry into the home, the place of rest. Electronic devices from cell phones to laptops and desktops occupy every waking moment and apps intelligently profile and endlessly bombard life at every turn and beeps during sleeping times, invading life, and demanding attention. This is noise that distracts and pulls meaning away, blinding who we are and the beauty of life.

All around I see many who refuse to sit still and listen to the voice within, to confront life and see themselves and the paths pursued, that amount to shallow parallels of somebody else's dreams and aspirations and not those that are uniquely individual and beautiful. Public enemy number one, a powerful Mexican drug lord, hits the evening news and all my brothers in the house of steel gather around the television to see their idol that chased the ideals of their hearts. Everyone can see the drug lord looks pale, half dead, tired, and void of any meaning and substance and caught hiding in a hole. I know with certainty that if this drug lord had a chance to openly speak about his life, that he would tell everyone they would never want in a million years the weight of emptiness in his heart and the troubles that now pound him hard into the grave. The world body of law enforcement are all on him, there is no turning back, life is over, the grave is where he will lay.

In the house of steel, a perfect place to hear a Voice in silence, the brothers are watched in times of play. No one wants to sit still and listen. Their play reveals the desires of the heart. Playing a guitar, the life and times of wild parties are relived. The strings of the guitar are pulled to the tune of a firing gun, slapping slippers on the floor to sound like automatic weapon fire, and baby powder lines are cut and residue left on noses to simulate cocaine use during a wild party. Anything to fill time and occupy the mind to prevent the voice that will emerge in silence, that will make them confront the inner workings of the heart. Ironically, the brothers want different but refuse to sit still and listen to the call of love, for life that is different.

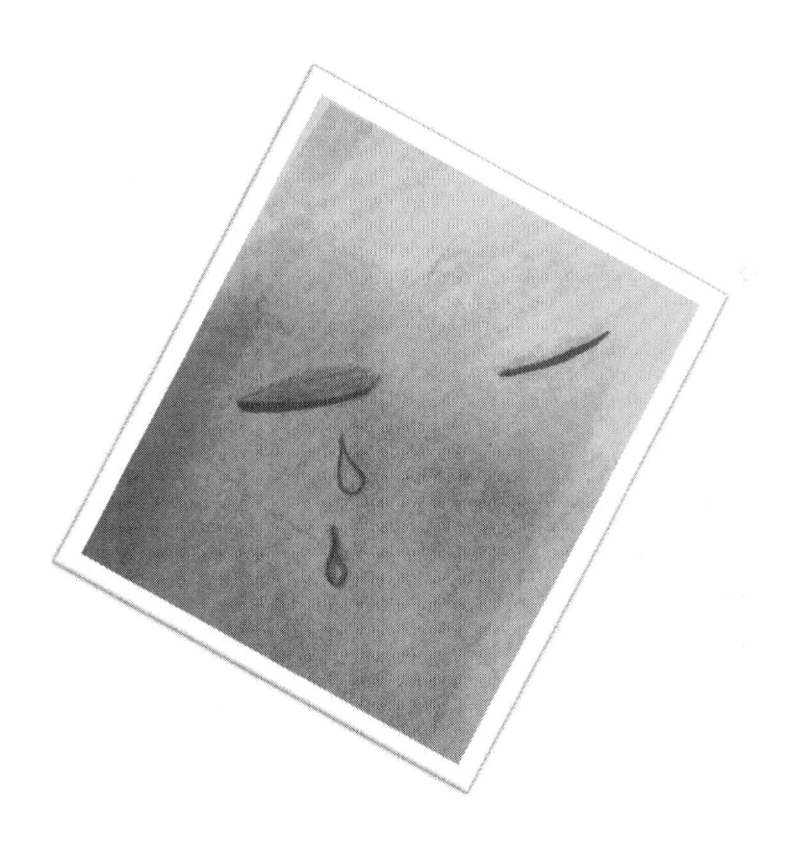

12

"Pain can become poetry. Poetry is our most personal use of words. It is our way of entering into the experience and bringing beauty out of it."

Gregory P. Schulz[vi]

Pain is all around, touching many people. The effects revealed through physical scars and those of the heart, the badges that riddle the surfaces of our skin and lives, medals of pain and hurt, some of which still throb and ooze. When the true costs are tallied up, generational boundaries of confused and lost lives, broken families and relationships, and damaged souls have been crossed. As pain in my life and in the lives of the brothers in the house of steel was reflected upon, I profoundly saw that all the hurt and evil being done by those who are dearest did not amount to my own sins that covered a lifespan. It was then that I began to see the wisdom of pain, and the beauty of people who are

on the same plane of life. All of us journeying on in life trying to figure it all out amid failures and victories here and there. Pain was no more an excuse to rebel, or to run away or withdraw from, or a justification to hurt or hate, or an experience that will pass. Pain was a source of beauty because with the tears inner wisdom of life emerged. Meaning through healing, life emerging in a form of hope, the strengthening of faith and the growing in the wisdom of love. Seeing pain through the life of another or my own gave a deeper understanding and appreciation of what it means to be human. We fail, make mistakes, and disappoint. But all of us are still beautiful, unique, and individual.

Given free and unprecedented access to all the brothers, many scars were seen. Severed limbs, half faces, blindness, scars across the throat, are all silent testimonies that speak of the destructive paths taken in the struggle to understand individual identities or to overcome pain and hurt. Lost lives all trying to discover the treasures of life through the chase for meaningless ideals that only serve to bring us further away from who we truly are. And all the battles outwardly fought only thickened the skin to weather the storms of life rather than have peace with it all from within. Jail strips everything away. Each person is naked and given a federal identification number for a name, a green jumpsuit and treated all the same, male and female, gay and straight alike. And the markings on our bodies and hearts, the scars and tattoos, are windows of individual journeys, not hidden in the shadows of the many clothes we wear to hide behind, such as fancy cars, money, gangs and guns! The house of imposing steel, bars of iron, and thick cold concrete, the dungeon of the contemporary world, showed how similar I was with everybody else. We were all hurting and broken.

All around I gazed into the hearts of hundreds, even thousands, of brothers that have so much pain that paralyzes them. All at once hurt is seen deep and life-affecting that I cannot help but see it as a reflection of my own life that has been easy when compared to many in the house of steel. There was a brother with one eye, the other was lost when a bullet struck the side of his face. The exposed scar covers many areas of his skull that is oddly shaped from the wound, a telling message of how fine the line between life and death. A hair follicle of movement in any direction at the time the bullet struck him was the fine line between this life and the next! This brother, Daniel, is a simple man, nothing complicated about him, whose only formal education is the third grade. The presence of his heart touched me with every encounter we had. There is a harmony about him even with the evil that materialized in his life. As he related his life story, I saw many of the Divine intuitive encounters that he spoke of in my own life. To me, this made the crossing of our paths already beautiful. What intrigues me about Daniel is that he does not listen to the voice of love that is without a doubt speaking to him and he hears and instead chooses to listen to the voices of the world that clearly scarred and driven his life. Evil can be very pronounced and public such as through a murderous act or as subtle and very inconspicuous through a statement that simply says, "You are not good enough." There are so many varieties of this statement: "You're not handsome or beautiful enough"; "you are too fat or too skinny"; "you are gay", "you have a big red nose." The list is endless, and such statements can and do wound. And Daniel, being gentle and simple, is affected by an in the face real world that tells him he is not good enough because he reads and writes at the level of a third grader. Daniel does not know how to hate, even the person behind the gun that took the side of his face and head off. In fact, this does not bother him. What does, are the many voices that tell him he is not good enough in so many ways. As I speak with Daniel, I am intrigued by how truly inter- and intra-personally intelligent he is, way above the average Joe or Jane. He reads people and situations so well that he could split a hair follicle in one, one thousandth of a second to avoid death when a bullet took the side of his face off. If that were anybody else, he or she would be in the other side of eternity.

Another brother named "Little One" is a young mischievous heathen who spent most of his life behind bars, not knowing who he is. As a young boy, Little One was taken into the United States by parents who are Mexican nationals living in America with false identities. Little One went to American schools and was raised in foster homes. He then finds himself being deported for committing a felony and then in jail for illegal entry into the United States. In his mind and heart, Little One is American even though the law says he is not. Little One's rebellion goes to the heart of who he is, American. And now he fights an impersonal federal system for his identity. Little One was watched staring at the ceiling for hours, frozen, confused about life. First a lost childhood, now an identity. This is a sad story to know, a profound invisible wound that goes to his heart and has clearly affected his life. As days passed, we talked of identity issues and a child began to emerge as each new day gave Little One confidence of who he is, perfect, beautiful, and Divinely loved.

Hope was borne for Little One the mischievous heathen, and love did it.

Another brother said his dad shot his mother in front of the sister in a murder-suicide when he was thirteen years old. When asked what in life he wanted, without hesitation he said to be with a sibling sister in Sacramento, California, and would be happy attending a parking lot for a living. Income of a parking lot attendant is less than ten thousand dollars annually without any type of benefits, nothing. I, on the other hand, worked as a maintenance supervisor making well over 70 thousand dollars annually with benefits and bonuses and all I did was complain. As I reflected further on this brother's life, the window brought my marriage and family into focus. I may have not committed a murder-suicide act, but there is a parallel in my actions that sent pain in the hearts of my whole family. My extreme drug addiction inflicted damage deep into the hearts of all involved. One day the brother came and out of nowhere says, "I hate fake flowers." Wondering where the statement came from, I pried for there was something significant about the comment. What came out next had me crying. The brother said, "I should have put real flowers on my mother's grave and drew her a picture." Drenched in tears, I held the brother and said, "Because this is your heart, consider it done." That day my angel Peanuts sent red balloons in the air alongside of the building where the brother and I were held. I told the brother the balloons are from him for his mother. The next morning the brother said, "Chris, the balloons changed color. They are blue." I smiled and said, "They did change color, Jesus sees your heart."

One evening a brother named Jose was outside my jail cell, gazing in. After a formal introduction, I invited him in. Jose is a man of few words and has a handicap of excessively long limbs although it was far from making him operate as a cripple. After a few moments, Jose was asked, "If God gave you a wish, what would it be?" After a long silence, tears began steadily falling, then he said, "To know how to forgive." The depth of this pain intrigued me. What was the hurt and who did he want to forgive? Apparently three guys stepped on his back and pulled his arms backwards, snapping them both as a grievous handicap hate crime. This was almost unbearable to hear. This brother's life-altering experience was serving as a mirror, to see how at one time evil plagued my life, when love was used as a weapon to carry out evil acts that only happened on Hollywood big screens. I remember finding out about numerous affairs the wife was having, not understanding why the hiding and fooling around had to continue as it did. Rather than simply walking away, the wife needed a justification for the marriage to end. To find justification, everything in the arsenal of evil was used, even love and a child.

Some pain is deep in the past. My youngest brother has a lot of hate towards me. One day he was told, and even given an opportunity, to take out his anger, to lay on the black and blue bruises at will. He was also told that the bruises will disappear, but the grief in his heart from inflicting pain will not easily go away, a reality that I know and had lived with. The violence in my own childhood, where pipes, knives and guns were used, taught me well about how the scars of the heart do not easily go away like the black and blue tattoos on the body. Hate leaves a deeper, lasting, and more destructive wound.

Invisible wounds of the heart can show up in hate, madness, and blame. These are abstract scars of the heart, much more severe than the physical wounds on the skin that heal. Hate, madness, and blame towards everybody and everything, with no personal ownership, is a heart separated from life, that thinks the world owes him or her something. The world owes nobody anything. We owe the world one thing, and it is sure to collect: A death! What is inside all of us determines who we are. In some weird way, the sins committed against us, the hurt inflicted by those who are the most special to us, are ours. Therefore, we can choose what is borne with it. We can make it destroy us by being a slave to it or we can make it be our servant as a powerful tool for positive change.

In the house of steel, thick scars that run the length of the inner forearm would be seen, clear signs of an almost successful suicide attempt, and I wonder. Heads concaved from a blow of a blunt object would be seen, and I wonder. Scars that went across the throat and that line the cranial crevices of the head, and even missing limbs would be seen, and I wonder. I would wonder about the story behind the battle of the wounds, the destruction of the parties involved. I would wonder about the chaos, the pain, the anguish, and the hurt in the hearts of these people, my brothers with me in the house of steel. One time a young brother was asked about his prosthetic right foot that was amputated below the knee. At first, I mischievously borrowed it and humorously began kicking everybody, telling everyone that it was the brother who owned the artificial foot. My joke was short lived for as I looked into the brother's red eyes it was clear he had an affliction that haunted him. He was mad at everybody, everything, the world. He was asked what it feels like, to which he said that his toes were always itchy and it felt like he had a very tight shoe on. This scared me. How do you relieve pesky itchy toes and a painfully tight shoe when there is not even a foot!

About a year after my arrest, I had a cellmate whose family was murdered in front of him by his nephew for money. On top of this, he was kidnapped by the Mexican drug cartel who used him to bury dead bodies, some of which had severed heads. While we slept, he would awake, yelling "Cucuey, Cucuey" as he covered his head and squirmed into a fetal position. Cucuey was the monster that made him re-live the murderous events of his family and visions of dead bodies with severed heads, the demon that haunted his nights while he slept.

Demons from the deep past haunted many of the brothers in the house of steel. There was another brother that had dark, deep eyes, with black circles around them, almost suggesting something within viciously lived. One day the brother came, saying he was being sexually assaulted by his cellmate, and was waking with semen in his mouth. Somehow, I knew that it was not true. For two weeks, he was kept at bay from beating his cell mate. And then, early one morning the recycle bin of aluminum cans made a crashing noise and on the floor were two brothers, one was the brother who was confiding in me with a CO on top of him, the other was his cellmate, knocked out cold by a sucker punch as he unsuspectingly came around a corner. It turns out that this brother snores and his cellmate would throw toilet tissue rolls at him for the snoring to stop. This woke the brother and a demon of his past, who relived a time when he was awakened as a young boy being sexually assaulted. This is a violation of the deep past, a demon that lingers, an open wound, a pain that has now become unpredictably destructive. I cannot help but see the long line of destruction that I caused in my own life because of the hurts I held hidden inside of me. The abuse of everybody important to me, including my own body with substance, were clear signs of how I let a demon destructively control me.

As I looked and saw the many brothers with scars, whether the scars were outwardly protruding or inner and painfully hidden, I could not help but appreciate the privilege that was given, even an honor, to partake in the pain and hurt that affected them by simply being trusted enough to be told about it. Together we cried, and sometimes laughed about it all.

Tears, laughter, and trust are my medals of honor from my brothers. Their life stories and experiences were the holograms with which my own life was superimposed, the common grounds of experiences that give wisdom behind the pain where beauty in some crazy way can be found. In love, we shared, through love we learned to trust again that life will flourish in the fertile ground where pain has decayed. The wisdom behind madness and hate, pain and suffering, gave life to a substance with which we could begin to love freely, fully, and unconditionally. My life has not been perfect, nor easy, but I can say that my heart and whole life is in a very beautiful place. Pain and suffering, affliction and bondage, are signatures of evil, all marks of the beast, a beast that Jesus Christ shut down at the Cross. The Lord has given me peace because I have given Him my whole heart and there along with it my pain and all my hurt. The good, the bad, and the ugly has now become my servants to do as I wish, to bring change not with brute force borne of human strength but by the Divine power of Love.

13

"These things I have spoken to you that My joy may remain in you, and that your joy may be full."

Jesus Christ

In jail, there is always noise. Alone and silent times are impossible. But some days the noise felt tranquil, surreal, and still as an inner peace was felt as my spirit connected with the Lord in an unusual way. The waving of hands, the movements of feet one step after the other, all seamless blends in a harmonic symphony, as if life naturally playing and nothing is out of place. At one end of the dorm, a brother strums a guitar, soothing tension in the air. In the middle of the room, brothers talking, laughing and joking, amidst the slamming and tingling of chips during a domino game. In the bathroom, a tapping razor of a brother shaving. And all-around brothers move about, feet and arms swaying, sending airwaves that clothe everything and everybody in repeating layers of soothing air. Hanging from the fire sprinkler red piping, are laundry clothes drying, swaying, as a brother has a make-believe boxing match with a phantom fighter. Jabbing victorious blows, wiggling body and head in an all-out brawl of silent phantom fighting, swaying to avoid knockouts from air-filled clothing.

Off in a corner I sat one morning, watching three brothers play scenes from the Three Stooges. From my silent perspective, eyes were seen being gorged out, thrown to the ground and stepped on, and imaginary wands were making people disappear. Tucked in a corner hiding by the laundry carts a brother jumps out and scares an unsuspecting brother jogging the rotunda who does not know whether he is in fight or flight mode, confused, and trying to do both at the same time because he is too surprised from the jumping, chasing bandit. Watching all this from my corner of silence I hilariously laugh, pray to have someone sit beside me and laugh too because everyone was looking as if I were some crazy person hilariously laughing alone in a corner. And then God sends a brother over, suggesting for me to write a letter to God about what was so funny. I laughed even harder at how God was poking fun at me with His

unusual sense of humor. Then, "Little Bull," a Spanish brother, sits beside me like a puppy wanting to be pet, wagging his tail, smiling in his peculiar way, asking for sugar and banana cheese cake that he had seen me make with the morning's haul of bananas that many of the brothers collected for me on Thursday mornings. Little Bull is a cheerful brother with his body always four steps ahead of his thinking!

"They seldom reflect on the days of their life, because God keeps them occupied with gladness of heart."

King Solomon

My grateful heart, my joy and peace, ran deep in the dungeon of steel, and told me I was in the "promise land." The keys to the steel door that led to the sidewalk outside would have provided no more freedom then I already had. I was free on the inside. I loved life right where I was, and it was hard seeing the problems with the law that was trying to impose upon my heart. One morning before "wake up" call I sat at a corner table listening to music, worshipping, reflecting on life, with two other brothers. All of us were lost in deep contemplation as we blankly stared at an orderly cleaning the bristles of his push broom, losing ourselves as our minds drifted off in the silent ambiance. There was a stillness in the air, and a

seamless blend of air and sound waves, and subtle, slow motion body movements. A symphony, a harmony song with the instruments of life, the notes in our hearts and thoughts, a harp of hearts being played by angels saying, "Peace be with you." Despite all that was going on with all of us, despite the United States' justice department against us, despite the prison bars of iron and cold imposing steel all around us, and despite the uncertainty of many aspects of our lives and families, there was one thing for certain, we were at peace in our hearts and all that was going on in our lives. Through this peace, we all were being ministered to. Even though the times were uncertain, we knew the Lord was organizing and filling the compartments of our hearts, harmonizing us to the tune of His Love.

Christmas Eve, 2015, all broke program rules to stay up for Santa and the gifts he wrapped for all the brothers in our range. Santa, in this case, was Peanuts my angel who gave the funds to buy the gifts for all at the commissary. With $40 dollars, candies, cookies, chips, socks, pens, paper, and all sorts of gifts of heart were wrapped and placed under our humble cardboard cut-out Christmas tree. Love alone brought harmony and peace in the brother's heart that Christmas Eve. They were singing, telling jokes and laughing, and having playful blanket parties while they waited in anticipation for what Santa got them. There was great joy in the air, and the whole floor wondered about the jolly, jingle bell rocking that was happening in our range. The gesture of a gift went deep for all knew that even though it was a ramen noodle soup or a pencil, it was given as a gift of love and gratitude of who they are, a beautiful creation. A simple 3-foot cardboard cutout tree decorated with plastic sporks, chip bags, soap pouches, toothpaste tubes and cut strips of plastic bags carried a presence, a settling peace despite very uncertain and chaotic times for all of us. The tree was unauthorized but parades of commanding officers and secretaries came and gave heart-felt reviews, even the director of the institution came to see our tree of love.

Never once did I find myself trying to occupy time merely existing while in the house of steel. Life was being lived to the full in jail. Many things brought amusement, and the Lord was intriguing me in the many ways He was speaking and the humor with which He was using. Freddy, a jailhouse barber, who just happens to be half gorilla in my opinion because of all the long facial hair on him, was cutting hair one morning. I saw all the brothers coming out of the barber room completely bald and when I walked in, there is Freddy. In a bald plague of irony, all the brothers were coming out of the barber room with no hair while the barber was full of hair! I laughed, and said, "Freddy, this is the craziest picture to look at," and off came all my hair, too!

In the dorm, a giant nuclear roach makes a mistake and begins traveling across the range floor, catching the attention of the tallest prisoner in the federal correctional system. "Flaco,"(Spanish for skinny) all 7-feet something inches of him, leaps to his feet intently focused on this roach as he grabs an empty plastic cereal bowl and flips it on top of the critter. Taking a plastic spork, the giant Spaniard repeatedly and rapidly taps the spork on the container over the roach and traumatizes the pesky critter while he did some giant Spanish conquistador victory dance around his captured roach. After lifting the plastic bowl, it was clear the sorry roach was dazed and confused. And no sooner did it begin to move, over again does the plastic bowl come down and the goliath Spaniard begins his percussion pounding torture, traumatizing the roach and doing his conquistador dance of victory in conquest! The giant Spaniard was going to fight another brother one afternoon and was told he could only fight brothers that were his size. With this standard, he would never fight because all my Mexican brothers with me in the house of steel were four foot tall or shorter!

Another brother named "Koko" would have an intense conversation with the shower every morning, cussing and yelling at the top of his lungs. I always wondered what the argument was about, whether it was about the water being too slow or the temperature not being regulated I do not know, but there was a rumble going on in the shower and it had something to do with the water, waterman or the water bill! And then, the brother would walk out as if nothing happened. This was always a morning, looney's tune, funny favorite.

One day four brothers had a slug fest and chair-swinging fandango that even the commanding officer would not dare get close to, and instead hits the panic button and dumps canister after canister of pepper spray at the brawling brothers. This rumble had been brewing for a week already because the kitchen orderlies kept stealing too many chocolate chip and blueberry muffins and the morning meal service was continuing to come up short so the brothers began handing out black- and blueberry eyes! The next morning, I could not help but poke fun at the CO who pepper sprayed the brawling brothers and the rest of us on the floor. With the CO listening, I jokingly asked the brothers if they heard about a new soda product at the commissary. Almost simultaneously all asked which one? I said, “It’s not Sierra Mist but CO Pepper Mist, not carbonated and sparkling but airborne and very irritating, and you don’t have it with lunch or dinner rump roast but with an all-out jailhouse rumble." The CO, quick to respond, said he would gladly empty more canisters of pepper spray if we all would like since it would especially be easier for all the reports were done and all that was needed were name changes. Of course, all of us on the floor declined, for all gagged and itched for hours while locked in our cells with the amount of pepper spray released the day before and knew the crazy CO would do it again!

One day a brother with some psychological issues was invited to have some "humble pie." Upon giving him the pie, he was asked to be honest about how the it tasted. With an expression that could not be read, the brother says “The pie smells like old people and taste nasty but because he respects me he was going to eat the pie.” I laughed so hard at his candid honesty. Of course, my curiosity peaked and I had to know if the brother was pulling my leg with his comment, especially since I was good at reading expressions but for some reason, in this case, I could not tell if his words were nothing other than the truth, that the pie "smells like old people and tastes nasty." The pie smelled like strawberry cookies, the flavor used to garnish the pie. After telling this to the brother, he just candidly said, "It smells like old people" as he ate more pie. Laughing even harder, but still not convinced of anything other than what he was telling me. Inquiring further, the brother insisted on his initial statement and said because he respected me he was taking the rest of the pie home to eat. If this brother was lying, he is the greatest hustler in the world because I truly felt guilty for sending him home with pie that "smells like old people and taste nasty!"

Another brother one day said the following: "Chris, I was hungry and asked God why He feeds the birds and wild animals and not me. Instead, He sends a wild pig that chases and tries to hurt me. I also asked God to keep me out of trouble and instead sends a cat that keeps getting in my way that I had to kick it four times before it left. Now I am in jail for illegal entry into the United States." As I was told this, I laughed so hard it hurt, and everybody in the room thought I was crazy and could not understand my laughter. I told the brother that I had my knife and fork ready to eat because his food was chasing him and all he had to do was turn around, kill it, cook it, and have a heavenly feast. But because the pig was not prepared for him to eat, he said God did not answer his prayer. Further, God put a cat in his way to change his direction but instead he kicked the cat and now he is in jail and he says God did not answer his prayer. Finally, I told the brother that in all his rebellion God did not desert him, for now God has given him his way, he has three square meals warmly prepared for him every day and twenty-four hour a day presidential guard to keep him safe and out of trouble!

Before giving a sermon on Babylonia the seductress one night, the girls met in the sex industry were reflected upon. They would enter my house and I would complement them on their beauty, referencing more their hearts rather than their natural beauty. They would say I was crazy, and I would tell them that I am not the one going into a stranger's house at 2am in the morning. This statement should be a footnote but is turning more into foot-in-mouth for I am not sure why it is even being mentioned.

Anyway..., as I related to the brothers the images that ran through my mind as verses in Isaiah 3 were read, all the while laughing, the brothers, about 30 of them, thought I was crazy and in need of medication, wondering what was so funny. It may have been that the information was not being related properly. Whatever the case, there was a wellspring of joy flowing from my heart as the end game of Babylonia the seductress was spoken about. Vivid imagery was flashing about what will happen to the harlot that enslaves many hearts. "Instead of fragrance there will be stench." In other words, instead of enticing perfume, rotting flesh. Going further, "Instead of a sash, a rope," meaning a noose around the neck and hanging in the gallows. "Instead of well-dressed hair, baldness; instead of fine clothing, sackcloth; instead of beauty, branding." Nobody was following my logic and laughter. There was nothing but blank looks and empty faces.

And then, a crazy happens. I found myself being cuffed and hauled off to the SHU, the Special Housing Unit, for being in an unauthorized area. That area just happened to be my cell, which had been home for seven days already but the commanding officer insisted I was sleeping in the wrong cell! Across nine physical head counts that ran the span of seven days and I was found to be missing finally! If this is the case, not one CO needs to be fired but every one of them across the whole United States Federal Bureau of Prisons!

14

"Peace I leave you; my peace I give you. I do not give as the world gives."

Jesus Christ

Steel, steel, steel. Lots of it, every geometric shape and angle, thick, cold, and imposing, begging to threaten individual sanity. Welcome to the SHU, the Special Housing Unit, a place used for discipline. It is the heart, the core of the fortified house of steel in downtown San Diego. The dungeon of dungeons, where the steel does not get any thicker anywhere else in the Metropolitan Correctional Center. The very intention of the structural design of the SHU is to impose psychological confinement through physiological means. The environment is sterile, with no mental stimulation whatsoever. Imposing steel blankets every square inch, yelling, "I will break you!"

But this only works on an individual that is not free, free from the bondages of the world, the paralysis of yesterday's mistakes and tomorrow's lost possibilities. All of this constricts the mind and heart, and hence present life in the now, where all true possibilities exist, kinetically stored, waiting to be borne. The steel had an opposite effect, a positive presence that provided a peaceful silence that exuded the fortitude of the Lord's Spirit, angels encamped roundabout with wings of impenetrable peace.

Heavily chained, three officers provided escort to a cell, number 8-3. The number brought a smile for it was an 11(8+3), the Lord making His presence known. A calm settled deep within as the door was locked, and notice was taken of the new mattress and of how clean the cell was. Seventeen months in the jail and sleeping in at least ten different beds and never once was a new mattress slept on or a clean room seen and now an immaculate one was stood in. My smile grew wider, the joy a well-spring as the Lord's fingerprints and signature were recognized, a voice speaking forth in the silent ambiance. Mischievously, joy overfloweth within, for being in the SHU felt like 5-star executive service because now not just one, but three commanding officers were literally and figuratively providing hand and foot service. Literally, in that any movement that required the unlocking of any device on the cell door entailed shiny iron bracelets and anklets be placed on my wrist and ankles. And figuratively, all meals were brought by members of staff and not inmates and showers had three fully armed escorts. This was 24-hour, VIP presidential guard and executive service and it felt good being the president!

The steel box provided a fortitude of peace that no demon that lurked outside could enter or imposing cold iron disrupt. The metal was fruitless against a free heart and spirit that left through every crack, opening, and key-hole at will! Three days in the SHU and the steel dungeon had zero effect on the spirit or heart. The body, after three days without a shower, was smelling like a horse, however. When a shower finally happened, the water was either freezing cold or scalding hot with no temperature regulation whatsoever. This, too, is another feature of the SHU designed to break the spirit of a person. But like the ineffectiveness of the imposing steel that withers against a free heart, so, too, does the scalding or freezing showers just ripple away along the surface of the skin, bringing laughter, smiles, and inner joy rather than madness, rebellion, and further broken heartedness!

Although the SHU is nothing compared to the mildew and feces-stricken dungeon that the apostle Paul was chained during biblical times, the glory of God within Paul's heart was no different in mine. Two amazing things happened. First, jail cells were changed, from 8-3 to 7-2, a 9! This was God again. Laughing and smiling wide while being placed in the cell, the three CO escorts gave inquisitive looks, their expressions saying everything--this man has lost his mind! Once the cell door was shut and the rattling chains and brass keys for the royal jewelry settled, another glory showing happened and set the tone that personified living, in real-time, through the symphony of hymns that played in the dungeon that St. Paul was chained. Across the ventilation system, considered the SHU's wireless telephone network, music carrying a glorious ambiance emerged from the floor above. The females gathered in worship and sang in perfect synchronization the melodies of their hearts. The renewing of their spirits could be felt. A glorious, heavenly throne sound, ambiently reverberating throughout the range, a harmony in sound waves passing seamlessly through the thick steel and reaching every cubic inch of space and penetrating the heart and soul. Angels saying, "Holy, holy, holy, is the Lord God Almighty. The whole earth is full of Your glory" (Isaiah 6:4). This was the Spirit of the Lord saturating the atmosphere with peace, grace. Tears flowed steadily, in eternal gratitude for warm and gentle love.

Nobody was in jail, and no cold steel was containing free hearts in this house of fruitless iron bars and chains. All were freely floating about in the refuge, strength and wings of angels. And the thunder, lightning and dark clouds outside only added to the glorious ambiance within, amplifying the presence of the Divine. Peace reigned. As the ladies sang their hearts out, their fears melted away, their hearts abundantly renewed. All mutually felt this Divine power. Everything that was trying to impose itself on the mind and heart melted away.

"Many lamps were burning in the upstairs room where we were meeting."

Acts 20:8

As the apostle Paul gave the sermon in the "upper room" after the "fellowship meal," the power and peace of the Spirit can be felt through the scriptures. Many lanterns were envisioned, with the darkness of the room blending away in the background, and the glow, the ambiance, on the believer's faces is the reflection of hope, love, and peace that filled all their hearts. There is solemn peace, beautiful, majestic, and glorious, that all could not be disturbed by the chaotic times outside of bloody persecutions, beheadings, and martyring of believers. St. Paul, and all in the "upper room" with lanterns, were surrounded with a wall of grace and peace that penetrated everybody, even those of us 3000 years into the future.

As the SHU ventilation echoed the hymns of the females worshipping, I floated peacefully to sleep, a solemn and restful sleep. There was a stillness, a silence in the air the next morning, saying that nothing in time, space and life was out of place. Something far greater was in supernatural control and powerfully working. And then, the Divine emerges in the air through a brother solely and solemnly singing with depth of heart and soul. From another range in the SHU, an individual silently, softly, and very peacefully singing, pouring his heart out to the Lord in the early morning silent air, creating a glorious ambiance. Very powerful and consuming. The brother's symphony of heart seamlessly echoing through the wavelengths of the air, the walls, the heavy steel, nothing stopping the comfort it brought to the heart. The solemn chant withers everything in its path, even pain, hurt and broken heartedness. There is nothing in all the world that can fabricate or create such powerful evidence and testimony of Jesus Christ in our hearts, lives and world. Very real and powerful, consuming, peaceful.

The SHU was a blast, a glorious blast. And the fun was just getting started. A CO comes by each cell handing out commissary sheets. Getting one, a pencil was asked for but the guard pays no attention and walks off. How is the sheet supposed to be filled out without anything to write, I thought? A brother in the next cell heard the request for a pencil and said he had one. Of course, I naively asked how to get it for there were a thousand locks and a foot of steel to get through before anybody could walk to the neighbor's house asking to borrow some brown sugar! The brother tells me to tear a line from the bedsheet and tie it to a toothpaste tube and throw it out the bottom of the door where his line would be waiting. It was game on from this point forward, for the door of the kingdom of heaven just opened in the thick steel dungeon. The Lord awakened childhood memories of lonely fishing trips on a beach, only now it was fishing expeditions in the heart of the house of steel. The fishing lines in the SHU figuratively opened all the locks to the doors and dropped the chains to the floor and every person was going in and out of their cells and meeting in our front yards where all were playing.

Commissary bags came and the sharing of love through the Ministry of Food had begun in the dungeon of dungeons. With fishing lines baited up with everything from coffee and sugar to oatmeal, ramen soup, beans, and summer sausage to medicine, the trolling began across the floor as items went into different cells. Just as a fishing line was cast out as a kid and pulled in with a fish, so, too, were the lines in the SHU. Big fish were being caught! One brother, who lived in the cell diagonal across, had impressive fishing skills. No matter what cell he threw his line to, even if it was right beside him, which was the hardest target, the line made it into the cell on the first try. Whether this was natural talent or experience from being in the SHU too long was not known, only that it was amazing to watch and beautiful to be a part of. This was not jail, nor was it the SHU. This was Heaven.

As commissary items trailed across the floor in impressive great oceans distances of the world, laughter could not be contained about the amusement the commanding officers in the control room were having as they watched the high seas fishing expeditions on video surveillance. The laughter must have been heard for jangling keys rang, signifying a CO was on the move. And there in the middle of the wide-open floor, in the most obvious place, is a line with a supermarket attached to it. All lines stopped moving to not call attention to the items, an inconspicuous attempt to hide the elephant in the middle of the room, myself frozen amidst laughter that was so hard the belly was full of labor pains of joy! The CO never came and the fishing line with supermarket whale in tow continued its delivery to the cell diagonal across the way, through an "online" system of old school world wide web made contemporary through mechanical ingenuity. Everything made it into the cell except the last item, a beef summer sausage that had not been flattened enough to fit through a much thinner threshold that it came out of. In front of the door, stuck outside with no way in, lay the sausage. And behold, a female CO, the one that placed me in the SHU, stands towering above the sausage as a victorious triumphant conquistador and says, "What is this?" while looking at me, the head of the ministry of food in the jail that all knew about. Of course, with halo on head and smiling angelically, all involvement was denied. The CO then says, "You guys need to smash the wiener more" and walks off. All laughed and began the rescue and recovery mission of the now miracle sausage that should have gone into the dark abyss of hell--the trash can! There were lines crisscrossed in every direction, coming from every cell to tie the sausage up in knots somehow to get it home. Nothing worked. Finally, after an hour of fruitless attempts, a t-shirt as a drag net was made and the wiener was yanked through the tiny threshold opening. All had just got done playing in the front yard. The time, 8:57pm (8+57=65=6+5=11). The cell number the sausage went into, 6-3 (9). Wow, a 9:11, Jesus and His angels had just watched a movie with great joy.

Fishing and whaling expeditions in the dramatic oceans in the dungeon of steel was proving to be fun, much more than the waters of the Pacific Ocean as a young boy. But now it was time to cook the catch of the day without a campfire, ancient cooking implements or 21st century utensils of spoon, knife, or fork. The brothers all asked what was on the menu. And smiling, with heart filled with joy, all were told not to worry but to know the menu was going to cross the Pacific Ocean and go into international destinations that included Mexico, France, and the United States. Looking to heaven, I prayed for the Lord to inspire a recipe for the limited ingredients and resources available. And an inspiration came. A banana cream pie, crepes and burritos were to be made with a banana, honey bun, an apple, a Hershey's chocolate almond bar, chicken flavor ramen noodle soup, banana creme oatmeal, a packet of mayo, a piece of chicken steak from lunch, flour tortillas, and jalapeno cheese. I smiled at the Lord, for this was not going to be an easy task.

Three hours later the Lord's three course international gourmet meal was announced as being ready. Out came fishing and whaling equipment and charter boats to deliver foods from around the world through the cracks and crevices of the triple locked steel fortress and across the open seas of white tile floors carrying delicacies of international and Divine cargo to hungry and eager brothers who marveled at the miraculous wonders before them.

The experience in the SHU ranked the very best time in the house of steel. And if this two years' period in the house of steel were the most beautiful times in life thus far, then being in the SHU takes the award-winning prize, the Oscar, of my life. How ironic, it is supposed to be the worst living and constricting conditions ever stayed in.

While the boundaries of joy had fallen in the steel dungeon, rumor of the "Iron Chef" in the Ministry of food was circulating the floors of the Metropolitan Correctional Center. Rumor had it that I had gone crazy

after smoking spinach and tried to strangle a CO and that was the reason for being placed in the SHU. If there were any rumor running loose in my life, this would be the one that I would like to take the prize!

15

"As he spoke, the Spirit came into me and raised me to my feet, and I heard him speaking to me. He said: Son of man. I am sending you to the Israelites, to a rebellious nation that has rebelled against me; they and their ancestors have been in revolt against me to this very day. The people to whom I am sending you are obstinate and stubborn. Say to them, 'This is what the Sovereign Lord says.' And whether they listen or fail to listen—for they are a rebellious people—they will know that a prophet has been among them."

Ezekiel

Before being arrested, every federal law enforcement agency in the United States plagued my life. Homeland Security agents, postal inspectors, DEA, ICE, BATF, and every type of federal informant and K-9 unit had already been following and sniffing around for at least two years. There was nothing said, done, or looked at that the law did not know about, and no place that they did not follow, even the information

highway of the World Wide Web and wireless telecommunications. At the post office, inspectors asked for mail pieces and parcels to be opened. On an airplane, x-rayed. Off the plane, questioned about money and drugs and then searched on the sidewalk outside. Go to the store, and business suddenly picked up. A crowd always followed everywhere. In a bright orange Chevy Camaro, drove everywhere at a 130mph all day and night and nothing happened! It was the craziest thing. State and city police would attempt to pull me over and then suddenly their red and blue lights would turn off and they would disappear!

Blue-Shoes came on the scene after I had walked away from a criminal life that still had its chains around my neck through the strap on my arm to expose a vein and inject crystal meth, through the money at my disposal, and through the fornicating shame with the seductresses in the sex industry. Blue-Shoes looked, looked hard, and looked very deep into my life, saw, and knew every deed that I had done, and continues to look up to this very day! My criminal life was over way before the law had come, and before their eyes they have seen how a shattered life began its journey of deliverance, from darkness and shame to light and the confidence of love. And yet they fail to believe what they have seen--change and miraculous transformation.

Blue-Shoes did not stop when the steel cage was entered. Waves of federal operatives playing both sides of the law were looking for an easy way out, a get-out-of-jail-free card, and they thought I was the ticket to a lighter sentence if a jailhouse confession could be obtained. God did not make a dummy. While many were looking for an easy way out, Jesus was sought in a challenge to love and not harbor hate for an enemy who wanted blood. To be an example of a different freedom was the desire, a freedom from the prisons of the heart, a freedom from whatever held the Blue-Shoes brothers as slaves. And to affect them, meant to love them in truth. This was not easy. Discerning trickery and trap, federal informant or jailhouse snitch, was not the challenge. It was responding in truth, in sincerity of heart amidst people who wanted blood. If someone was being called brother, then this better not be a cheap and shallow address. Everyone, no matter who they were or the reason they were near, was an opportunity given by God to plant even a small seed of love in a hurting heart.

Many took my faith and giving heart as a weakness and constantly thought they could get incriminating evidence through a jailhouse confession. To them, Chris was the ticket, the get-out-of-jail-free card. This was of great personal challenge in the truth about love. The Lord was constantly sought, to have Him direct the heart with the message of love and not hate. Blue-Shoes did not only disregard the message but also refused to see and acknowledge the miracles that happened before their eyes. These miracles were real, very observable, and individual, speaking directly to the hearts of the brothers, to follow and trust truth and not empty promises of freedom from federal prosecutors cutting deals for lighter prison sentences in exchange for incriminating testimonies. But miracle after miracle, message after revelatory message, truth after piercing truth, all of which had the undeniable signature of God, just trampled upon and disregarded by virtually all the Blue-Shoes brothers.

Many Blue-Shoes brothers lived a life through routes that played both sides of the law, and repeatedly found themselves in the very same position at which they started, in trouble and lost. This literally does not only pronounce crazy but defines it! They want freedom from the revolving doors of the steel cage and locked doors but do not even know what freedom is. To be free from the criminal life and the confines of prison walls is not through easy-way-outs-riding-on-people's-back but through a heart free of affliction and bondages that the self has built life upon. Brothers have been released early from jail, to go home and die because of terminal cancer. This is not freedom, it is death. Brothers have made the evening news after being released that day, only to climb to the roof of a building they stared at from their jail cell for six months and jump to their death. This is not freedom, it is fear. And brothers have been released early, only to go back to an old life that went nowhere. This is not freedom but the walking dead. Many believe that freedom is through the unlocking of doors in the steel cage or life as usual on the outside and not through Jesus and His love on the inside.

Even during times that the Blue-Shoes brothers were outside traveling the highways and city streets, they chased everything in their wayward and rebellious journey. Money, possessions, gangs, and guns are the pursuits of the world and our flesh, and these brothers bought into this philosophy and lived the American dream rich with pain, sleepless nights, and nightmares when sleep is found. Little did they know, they were not free then, nor are they free now, and will never be free until the lust and thirst for this world is replaced with love, love for the Lord and the individual and unique life He is calling all to sing. This is how my freedom was found, and where the inner longings of my heart were satisfied.

This is not a boast of being better or even holier. Battles rage within, and experience speaks from personal sorrow and pain of life once lived in the shadows and dark empty pit of shame. Why Lord Jesus has chosen to reveal Himself, I know not. What is known, is that the Lord is powerfully real, and there is no being quiet about His truth and voice that so beautifully calls in a gentleness that has never been known. To know Him, to honor His love in all creative capacities, and to do it with all my heart, is all that the heart desires. There are many voices in the world, calling to be one way and another, even religion saying Jesus is do this and do that. I refuse to listen to any of the voices as a choice to know the Lord. Knowing the Lord did not come by way of what someone has said, nor by what was read in any book, including the bible. Jesus Christ--and hence, life--is known by what He has done in my heart, by the miracles that have now become normal occurrences in everyday life, even in sleep through dreams. And it can be said with certainty that the Lord is not just revealing Himself to me. No. He is speaking and showing Himself to all through everything in all creation. The only question that remains is not that God exists, but why are we not listening and responding to His voice? He is loyal in time of need, gentle in times of pain, personal in times of loneliness, and humorous in silly and playful moments. Nothing compares.

Proclaiming to know God, then how can I be hating anybody? To "love my enemies, to bless those who persecute me," has proven to be a great challenge of faith, but also the most instrumental tool in the instruction of love, love not just in word but in truth and in sincerity of heart. The night Jesus was arrested, He knew Judas was going to betray Him and yet called him friend. If the ultimate sinner can be called friend, then my most evil pursuer can be called brother. It was painful to embrace someone who had evil intentions for being near, but it grieved the heart more to not care, knowing that the lost were not being helped. Many Blue-Shoes brothers were desperate and wanted freedom from the steel cage but clearly do not know what freedom is. Easy way outs of the house of steel through cooperation with federal prosecutors only served as a revolving door in a crazy cycle of sin and enslavement to what held them captive to begin with. Now, there is a federal correctional system that is bursting at the seams, ready to explode as it faintly manages a symptom and has not even remotely come close to addressing the problem. The real problem is broken hearts that are hurting, that wander the lost wayward roads of the world looking for life in all the wrong places, a life that can only be found through love, a love that transforms a heart, and that love is Jesus Christ. This is true freedom from the bondages and enslavement of sin that imprison the heart, and therefore, the life. Through my life, and the freedom that has been found, a door was offered to the Blue-Shoes brothers that no amount of chains and iron can contain.

My heart is free, my life moving about in a world that all around trap doors are seen with signs that offer life—wealth and material possession--but all that is seen from the lives that enter and come out of the doors is sadness, regret, and further brokenness rather than hope that stirs imagination, inspiration and even fantasy of the infinite possibilities of potential that comes with a free heart. Out of love for the truth, a lost brother was edified toward the direction of true freedom. Many were hurting, paralyzed with fear, staring at the ceiling, trying to hold families and relationships together, crying, and this was painful to watch. It seemed that nobody took anything shown to them, even the miracles that were performed for them to know that the Lord undoubtedly is real and waiting with open arms.

Just as Moses grumbled to God about the troubles with the Israelites, my pleas, my laments, to the Lord were with much greater and desperate passion. Pleads were not to get out of jail, but the questioning of a Divine being as to why wave after wave of Blue-Shoes were being sent, that did not want love but blood? How does anyone go to bed knowing they are trying to hurt someone they do not even know and has done nothing to hurt them? Pleading with God, why is this happening? Why can He not bring people that did not lie about being of the kingdom but were of the synagogue of Satan? Laments poured out and continued, telling the Lord that Blue-Shoes are thieves and robbers who are blind and dark, who follow their father the devil.

"The new man in you outshines the darkness all around. May those who live in darkness be drawn to Jesus, the light of the world who is in you."

Peanuts

All around it was hard finding brothers without evil intentions for being near. The floor was riddled with Blue-Shoes operatives trying to trick and entrap. This was a tremendous struggle, a challenge like no other in faith, for the heart that still had open and seething wounds was given always, only to have it

trampled upon. Heavy tears painfully filled and spilled out of the heart. Even though the experience was designed to strengthen faith and draw Jesus near, it hurt tremendously. Distress was twofold. Selfishly, it was hard to understand how anyone could go to bed knowing that their only intention for being around a person was to hurt the individual. This was high evil, and the Lord was saying to "love my enemy?" How? Why? "No, Lord, no" I pleaded. Then a revelation came. Is the enemy's greatest sin any different than even the smallest sins I commit daily? No! What hypocrisy! Secondly, how could anybody refuse all that Jesus Christ offered: Peace that settles the troubles of the heart, real hope, and transforming love that perfects all.

There was a Blue-Shoes brother that would always be close, and even though there were no doubts as to his intentions for being near, brotherly love and edification were always given. To prevent an elementary level trick to deceive by the brother, he was told that the steel walls of jail, the criminal case against him, and myself were road blocks that carried the voice of the Lord, saying to draw Jesus near and that there were no more get-out-of-jail-for-free cards being handed out. One day the brother spoke about the troubles with his girlfriend who wanted to separate. The girlfriend was struggling with the commitment of loyally and faithfully waiting seven years, and the brother was pressuring her. This was honorable of her not to commit to a decision that she did not mean at the time and needed space to deal with the issue in her own way and time. The Blue-Shoes brother was told to look at the evidence of her love, that she comes to visit, answers the phone when he calls, and her level of personal integrity by not being forced into a decision she wanted to freely decide on her own. All of this testified to her level of commitment to him and her heart.

At church that night, 9 brothers from the 11th floor attended service and the first prayer request was from an unknown brother asking to pray for spouses! In fourteen months of attending service, there was never a prayer request of that specific nature. Again, the fingerprints and signature of a Divine being making Himself known, speaking to the brother having girlfriend issues. And what happens? The Blue-Shoes brother hands the miracle back, choosing deception rather than truth to find freedom from the house of steel. "Freudian slips" of every form plagued the brother, revealing his evil intentions, adding insult to already injured heart. This brother spent massive amounts of time being near while I played the fool and overlooked his many attempts to get incriminating evidence about my case, giving chance after chance in true brotherly love. Now, I was making a Jesus9:11 call for guidance in a painful struggle to love the enemy. The following week Blue-Shoes lays on an all-out attack, for now there are teams of two wasting no time insulting and invading personal space. The emergency call to the Lord was answered with teams of invading Blue-Shoes brothers. Grumbling to the Lord throughout a restless night, furious and frustrated my body laid.

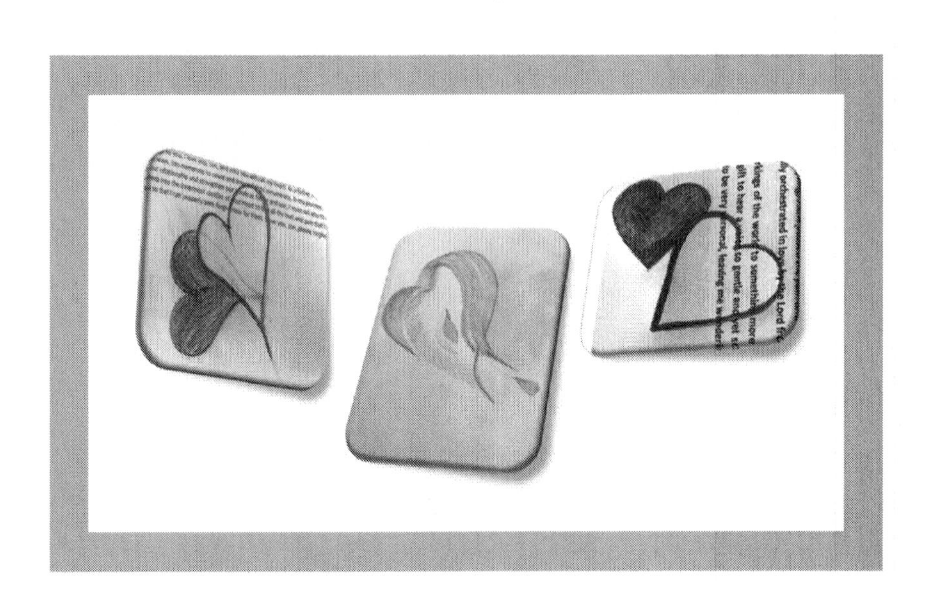

16

"No weapon formed against you shall prosper, and every tongue which rises against you in judgement You shall condemn. This is the heritage of the servants of the Lord, And their righteousness is from Me..."

"Because he loves me," says the Lord, "I will rescue him; I will protect him, for he acknowledges my name. He will call on me, and I will answer him; I will be with him in trouble, I will deliver him and honor him."

I Am

The prison chaplain, after praying, said, "Chris, the walls moved." This was troubling, for a dream occurred the week before of being on a boat floating on water with a wall in front that said, "The charges are dropped." The "wall" signified protection so when the chaplain said the wall moved it was understood as protection had been removed, which will never happen. With all the troubles that were happening,

protection removed was the last thing that needed to be heard by anybody, especially the chaplain in the jail. I prayed, saying, "Lord, I care not of the troubles, only of seeing You."

At the eleventh hour, fourteen days before the criminal trial is to start, many voices of evil began an all-out assault, tearing apart an already grieving and desperate heart. Voices from every direction were speaking hate, lies, deception, and my own voice calling for desperate measures to reexamine past mistakes to see if they have all finally caught up to me. And then, the Divine emerged. On the top and bottom of the page of my opened journal, the voice of the Lord comes through the thread of time from 2000 years in the past, saying, "I'm here, beside you, watching and protecting you as I have always" and "The Lord is good, a refuge in times of trouble. He cares for those who trust in Him"(Nahum 1:7). These Divine words bring comfort and consolation, settles the soul, and stills my spirit in the eye of the storm of my life. All that is known of the Lord, all that has been revealed through revelation, is real, true to the heart and therefore should be translated in the life. Even knowing this, I fail to remember that the Lord is forever working, in ways many times not seen. When there should be trust, there is flight from place of refuge. How foolish.

In the courtroom one day, a husband and wife were watched getting sentenced for drug smuggling. As the two met in the holding cell, one asked "How are the children?" then both of each other. The wife, strong and stoic, goes before the judge and returns crying, outcome not good. Husband goes in while wife waits in silence, a piercing silence that carries her whimpering across the way. The weight of the air tremendously heavy on my heart, too. That night, after mail call, two brothers were watched opening letters from their spouses, smelling the letters every other line, crying. This was touching to watch. Brothers gathered around the few that got letters, who openly shared the joy of love carried in an envelope. It was a beautiful moment, this love being passed from spouse to brother and by mere observance passed to me. In contrast, I could not help but remember the crying wife after being sentenced earlier that morning. This was a deep moment, sharing in silence, respectfully embracing in spirit.

Sleep came deep and peaceful that night. I wake early, finding a presence, a stillness, a state that has somehow been penetrated, a gift given from above. Then, a revelation comes. For many, the house of steel is the "valley of fear." All around there are many brothers that are paralyzed by fear. Many are struggling to understand their condition, to find the right words to say to a sentencing judge that will explain away all that has happened, the ultimate excuse and reason, and this eludes them, making them scared and even more desperate.

Many brothers came seeking advice, direction, edification or simply to share. Letters and photos, memories and moments, were all proudly shared, making me feel as one of their own, a loved one. How did this come to be? I have simply sought to be true to who I am and loved the Lord and striven to always strengthen my relationship with Him by being cognizant of His voice in everything, in the good and the bad, even the ugly. This sincerity of heart has translated in love toward all my brothers. The love for the Lord has been and will always be my confidence. The brothers see this but ironically cannot realize because it is a struggle of their minds to understand. Love is not something to understand but a reality of the heart. To understand is control. To love is surrender. This is the room of stillness and silence, a refuge in chaotic conditions, that was penetrated and is illusive sometimes. It is a refuge the brothers are trying to find in the "valley of fear." And Love is the key that dissolves the veil of fear and penetrates a room of peace. Opening this door requires abandoning the self and control, and many times understanding. The brothers see this door but refuse to relinquish control of their lives and therefore the shadow of fear holds them captive. But love allows the penetration of a state, that allows for an awareness of harmony that unfolds life in seamless, unhindered blends of experience, that transcends time, form, and space. As life happens, every experience, both negative and positive, become venues of opportunity to discover a dimension of love, to grow and become one with life, nature, and the Divine.

The human experience is a journey, a "pilgrimage," by which Love is revealed. Love is the looking glass to see, know, and experience the Spirit of the Lord in our midst. Love is a power to guide, instruct, and manage the heart every step in the journey further into the promise land, and is not a substance with which to try, but to live. There are no special powers. There is the power of love that brings inner peace and joy, that filters the noise and voices of the world, that keeps me true to who I am and singing my individual and unique song in the journey through life on this side of eternity. All our hopes, all our dreams, and the fulfillment of our hearts are found in love. Know Love, know life. When love is sincere, it is security, too. Love provides the wisdom and the strength to live and stretch through the good, bad, and ugly times. Nothing matters when love leads the way. Love demands respect. Respect for God, for the self, for life, for fellow humans and for nature.

All the events of the last five years are asking to hate in all that has happened, but it has not. On the contrary, I have learned to love, to love sincerely all creatures and life itself. Life has emerged through it all and made the journey beautiful. And the heart swells, even overwhelmed, when those who have desired evil are reflected upon. There is the law, forming and fabricating lies and liars to convict. Objectivity has been lost, justice subverted to promote a hidden, personal agenda. There is evil by those that are close and dear, that wish harm. All part of a web of intrigue to either help promote the injustice of the law or bring pain using love of a child as a leveraging tool. Evil will use any device as a weapon and will cleverly hide in a cloak of lies and subtle deceptive practice. There is lawyer subverting defense and playing both sides of the criminal justice divide. There are Blue-Shoes brothers playing both sides of the law, using trickery, abusing a sincere heart, and hiding in a false curtain of faith to be near, even being blasphemous by denying the miracles that have happened before their eyes and refusing to believe. To even innumerate all the evil

around is impossible, but the evidence through the actions of heart cannot be denied. This hurts deeply, grieves beyond measure, and yet all these voices of evil have not caused me to hate. I have grown in love and have had a fuller appreciation of life. No shadows haunt me or darken the way. I am free, for Love leads the way.

"The Lord said to Satan, "The Lord rebuke you, Satan!" The Lord, who has chosen Jerusalem, rebuke you! Is not this man a burning stick snatched from the fire?"

Zechariah, The Prophet

Once buried in sin and howling from the pit of shame that a life-long drug addiction provided, I now stand delivered by love. The soul was set for the fire but because the Lord loved despite my life salivating in sin, a voice was heard and called upon for different. Love lavishly embraced a broken heart and threw me out of hell. My heart is in a beautiful place, and life strengthened and confident like no other time before. Evil is looked upon in disbelief, that it is possible to exist in the levels in people's heart and deeds toward another. The wickedness is painful to know, but more grievous are the lost hearts of people that are captive to such evil. I wonder of the torment of their sleep. How do they hide from themselves and a God they

undoubtedly know exists, and sees? It is only hoped for them to come atop the mountain of hope, of joy, of life, free and full that is now lived, that is theirs too if only they dare reach out and call upon the Lord in sincerity and truth.

"And I myself will be a wall of fire around it,' declares the Lord,' and I will be its glory within."

Zechariah, The Prophet

A week before the criminal trial is to start and the early morning feels as if the mountain of troubles of the past five years has been crested. Then a vision happens. Looking up, a blazing fire round about was in the distance. There was darkness between, and glistening shadows and silhouettes moving about. Dressed in a priestly white robe with hands outstretched, looking to heaven while turning full circle, calmly gazing at what is before the eyes. Then, starting at my feet, a transparent white flame steadily burned upward. My figure is completely engulfed in white flame, and in the spirit looking on at the darkness round about being consumed by fire. Then intrigue happens as the Daily Bread devotional scripture for the morning is read, stating, "And as He prayed, the fashion of His countenance was altered, and His raiment was white and glistering," Luke 9:29, a

9:11! With all that was going on with the criminal trial and the flying arrows of the enemy, this morning was a glorious showing of the Lord, saying He is near, and there is great purpose for which He has protected-- Love.

Troubles all around trying to choke focus. At the height of this criminal ordeal, and to love amidst great evil, I refuse to move in desperation as the trial nears. Many miracles have happened, inherently saying that the path being travelled is correct, that finally things were going in the right direction no matter all the uncertainties that lay ahead. Remembering the miracles, the dreams, the visions, the voice of love every step of the way, and my slumbering spirit rose. Taking a handmade rosary hanging on my bunk, it was put on in a way like never before while staring out the darkened early morning sky through the iron bar window. Tears poured in rivers of peace, of gratitude. The Lord's presence was rich, and the manifestation of Love personified. Love is amazing, and the devil or anybody else that dare challenge my faith, that challenge love, will falter. Threats fly from all around, darkness surrounds, but a powerful force will divide the sea of darkness and provide passage right out the front doors of the dungeon of steel, far different from the basement back

doors of which the steel dungeon was entered. All will be conquered by fierce love. To those destined for testimony, glory. To those for fire, fire! All will see the sea of darkness parted before their eyes by a powerful strength of love and deliver a heart to the other side. The "Lord will not be defamed nor His glory given to another." This is promise, written in blood, confirmed with an immutable voice speaking loudly at the cross and Divine words written in time, coming alive 2000 years into the future.

By day's end, the Lord would give walking instructions. At church service that night, the sermon was on Mathew 28:16-20, the "Great Commission." What was intriguing were the numbers involved in the verses, they summed to 9(i.e. 16+17+18+19+20) and Jesus was commissioning the 11 disciples. Behold, a 9:11 appears. This was a turning point. The numbers and the sermon carried a Divine message, my walking papers, with instructions that read, "Go ye and make disciples of the nations." Any other day but this Sunday and timeframe in my life, these verses and even the sermon would not have been significant, intriguing or meaningful. Its timing was Divinely appointed to hear. On the verge of the criminal case ending, with the trial to start in two days, these two years in the house of steel has not only been a time of heart cleansing, life transforming, and amazing beauty, but also training ground for love. And now, the Lord commissions me with the anointing of His Spirit of love and its power. Having received Divine walking papers, the only question that remained is where I am to walk--outside the house of steel or into a prison cell for the next 20 years. The answer would come in less than seven days.

Slept peacefully the night before the trial and awoke remembering a dream and a voice testifying to the heart. And of course, my own panicking because of how the judicial system worked--it did not! Opening the Daily Bread devotional for the day, printed quarterly some six months prior, and the heading reads, "Be still." I laughed and smiled at this Divine humor. This is relationship, personal talks with the Divine each step of the way as trust deepens through the intrigue of testimony and revelation of the Divine. And then the dream was remembered. In the dream, a fat cow with a serious face was intently staring in a yellowish room. Suddenly, out of the cow's side a dwarf-like replica of the first cow emerged, intently staring again.

While waiting in penetrating silence outside the courtroom, the yellowish color of the steel room was noticed. It was the same as the one in the cow dream! Throughout the morning during court proceedings the meaning of the dream was wondered about. The judge began reading opening statements of the case that jurors were going to be told, saying "The case involves 45 defendants spreading across 10 indictments in an international drug smuggling conspiracy...." The United States attorney labeled the case "Crystal Palace II", and I was defendant 5 in one of the indictments. This case was the fat cow in the dream. This was a very serious matter, the "fat cow" intently staring me in the face! In a surprise move by the United States' attorney, a last-minute motion to suppress evidence was filed with the court. The evidence involved thousands of dollars in money orders that were administratively seized by United States postal inspectors who obtained a search warrant after a K-9 unit detected drugs in a paper-thin parcel that I mailed. According to my lawyer, the money orders were the biggest hurdle to overcome in the case. This big case, the "fat cow," had just miraculously turned to a dwarf cow with the largest body of incriminating evidence removed. The dream and the numbers involved in the case were intriguing. There were 45 defendants, a 9. The total amount of money orders seized and suppressed as evidence was $20,900(2+0+9+0+0), an 11! Behold, a 9:11 appears, again. These were Divine fingerprints, God saying He is in charge and knew all the time!

By evening of the first day of the trial, all the events were reflected upon. The sight in the courtroom was something. On the prosecutor's table were seven assistant district attorneys plus an army of support staff and special investigators. At the defense table, my attorney and me. The day that jury selection began, the morning began with an intensity never known or experienced, comfort could not be found. Looking around, intently listening for the voice of the Lord in anything, but only silence, a penetrating stillness. Pleads go up to the Lord who seems far away and nowhere to be found. Looking to the commanding officer who was securing me for transport to the courthouse and who the day before the Lord used to speak edifying words, he was asked for a word. And from the top of his head stated, "He that spared not His own son, but delivered Him up for us all, how shall He not with Him also freely give us all things?"(Romans 8:32). In tears, I said "Amen." This set the tone for the day.

On the threshold of this whole ordeal ending and the times are intense. Drug use with many near death occasions, loaded guns to the head, or bloody jailhouse brawls of warring brothers with prison shanks are all intense experiences, but nothing compares to the tidal wave of troubles that splash the shores of my life at this time. High evil all around that it is creepy. It's so subtle, but ever present and encroaching. Not to focus on this, but to capture it and show that nothing that comes against God's chosen will win. It is not about the devil, nor about the challenge or even the victory. It is about Love. To love, to trust, and to believe is the premise of faith. And judgement, the premise of fear. This is the line being contemplated as the criminal case came to an end. Was I trusting and believing, in a complete surrender of heart, or was a good game being played and that my fears were mistakes have finally caught up to me and a payment was going to be handed over in a form of a very long prison sentence? The work of faith was tearing deep into the heart, to remove all reliance of the self in a complete surrender and trust of Lord Jesus.

Intense it is, everything. Being in tight chains at the ankles and wrists the whole day in cold and imposing steel rooms and the weight of the air in the courtroom is hard enough. Now factor in the dirty little devil's doings in the background. Everything the federal prosecutor has presented is all scripted, made out during the investigation by the lead investigator and his band of federal informants working both sides of the law. Everything designed to use entrapment tactics by criminal operatives working with the federal government. I see my former roommate on video mailing a package loaded with drugs, making sure he is positively identified by facing the surveillance camera then slowly turning his face left then right. Then there are hours of wiretaps with individuals speaking in scripted conversations designed to incriminate another, me in particular! All these guys were caught selling drugs and guns to federal sting agents and have now cut deals with the government for lighter prison sentences in exchange for incriminating testimonies. It becomes very clear that the lead investigator has orchestrated the scripted lines for individuals speaking in the wiretaps. Over ten hours were played in the court room and none had my voice!

Earlier on before being arrested, while on crystal meth and life falling apart, a heavy undercover police presence was noticed everywhere I went. And in my stupidity, I started giving them an attitude. Curtains in my house were opened and crystal meth was smoked for all to see. While at a trolley station, a line of crystal meth would be cut atop a laptop and snorted in front of all, daring them to arrest, but arrest never came until a year later. All day and night long, sports cars were driven everywhere at 130mph, making personal roadways, and throwing money out of the window in the amount of the traffic violation, such as $402 dollars for going on the expressway without a passenger. This pissed Blue-Shoes off and it was no wonder why I found myself sitting in the defendant's chair charged in one of the biggest criminal conspiracy cases in southern California. Nothing, not even stupidity on crystal meth, justifies evil. In a perfect world, this would be true, but in our fallen state it is only an ideal of a perfect reality of a pipedream. At the end of every crystal meth pipe is a lot of trouble and broken lives. And so, I must learn to appreciate the lessons and the product of not only my own evil doings but those of another and learn to love in sincerity of heart.

Day three into the trial and the day began even heavier than the one before. The air, thick. The life, weighed, almost as if the whole world were a weight pressing the body into the ground with a pressure indescribable. Jesus is imagined in the garden of Gethsemane praying, knowing He was going to the cross carrying the sins of the world, blood sweat running down His face, an unimaginable pressure. As the marshal secured the leg irons, I complained of them being too tight as the locking device went click, click, click. To move, hurt tremendously, the irons tightened to be extremely uncomfortable. As the penetrating cold steel jewelry touched the skin, I could not help but think of the Lord being nailed on the cross, cringing at the enormity of the unimaginable pain, for me. My silence deepened. The marshal began her physical body search when the leg irons were secured. From the left arm, feeling very intrusively all the way to the wrist where she yanked and broke the shirt cufflink. I yelled, "Why are you treating me like an animal." Immediately the Lord's Spirit rebukes. Once again, the Lord was imagined being nailed on the wrists, I cringed at the pain unimaginable and indescribable. My silence grew deeper, for the Lord was silent while being nailed to the cross--For me!

Everything about jail is steel, lots of it, thick and very cold. On this day, the handcuffs, the chain around the waist, the leg irons, the steel bench, everything was freezing, a cold that penetrated the marrow of bones, making me fade and withdraw further into the self that seemed to get smaller and smaller as the cold reality of the evil that exists in the world began to further reveal itself. All that wanted harm could be felt mocking away from far off distances and from those who were near in the courtroom, echoing the slurs of the onlookers of Jesus hanging on the cross, saying crucify, crucify. Almost began to hate from the evil that was being felt, from the many who said they cared, but found myself grieving for those that follow darkness. Imagining Jesus on the cross, hanging, in great sorrow, grieving for those He loves. I asked myself what was crucified on the cross, love or evil? It was evil that Jesus crucified on the cross, using love, love for us who have grievously sinned against Him and each other.

Each day the trial progressed, the intensity of the pressure grew heavier, and there was nothing that stopped the pressing of my body into the ground. The Lord was asked to reveal the purpose of the intensity of everything. What was supposed to be known about the weight that was upon my life? Pleas to the Lord continued in the cold steel room where I waited in penetrating silence, but no answers came. The jury was expected to return an early verdict that would not be in my favor. They never came, but instead left for the day to return the following week for continued deliberations. Echoing in my head was the Lord saying, "I will sustain you and will rescue you"(Isaiah 46:4), scripture that was read early in the morning before court. I was having a hard time believing this, a horrible time living it!

All week the Lord was pleaded with, to remove the pressure, and the Lord has been merciful and gracious but living the essence of His promises was hard to sustain, difficult believing. The many miracles that have happened were looked upon. Jesus was thought of many times, of the pain and insult inflicted upon Him as the Roman soldiers hung Him like an animal on the cross and slew Him while bystanders yelled murder Him, murder Him, and this grieved me to see the evil for which the Lord went to the cross. And it is this same evil that is seen at work today, all around. So easy to hate, to hurt, to fight fire with fire, to fall into a practice that operates all around the world in many people's hearts. But no, only great sorrow could be felt for those who are lost and wayward, like me before returning to the heart of the Lord. The pain of personal suffering is known; I cringe imagining the pain the Lord suffered for me and how His heart now grieves for the evil that plagues the world. Then those who knowingly practice evil and sleep as if nothing is wrong are thought of. How tormented their sleep must be. Where is guilt? Where is conscience? What is life really like for those who refuse to empty their conscience, who make sin accumulate in the heart and who continue to hide behind lies and deceptive practices. Sickness and darkness haunt their lives.

Awoke heavy, the air thick, and the silence once again penetrating. With eyes closed, I began imagining leaving the house of steel, crying as my angel Peanuts drove me away in her car, being thankful and grateful. My eyes open and the pressure of the world comes to an even heavier reality. Although I see how far the Lord has brought me untouched and hold dear the sure promises of His love that is in my heart, I doubt and have a hard time believing, trusting Him. Comfort cannot be found and relief from the pressure only grew heavier with every moment that passed. All around, from my Daily Bread devotional to the bright shiny day outside to the remnant of joy deep within, all signs of the Lord's presence and embrace, and all that can be focused on was the evil in the courtroom, practiced by those who represent the highest law of the land, the Constitution of the United States of America. All is a fancy label, ideals of a pipe dream. All that was being practiced in the courtroom was a shameful perversion of our humanity, a sub-borne of evil cloaked in the guise of good, wrapped in a red, white and blue ribbon that stars the striped written lines of the Constitution of the United States, the supreme law of the land. Before God, all are naked, fully exposed.

"It always protects, always trusts, always hopes, always perseveres. Love never fails."

Paul, The Apostle

As the intensity of the troubles with the law relentlessly pressed, I looked around at the many ghost faces of my brothers, zombies of fear, paralyzed and frozen in a time capsule of yesterday, reliving mistakes that got the law breathing down their throats. I refuse to be contained by fear, for there is so much to learn, to swim through as an adventure of life just waiting to be discovered. Amidst all the pressure, pleas, in waves, went to the Lord, to apprehend the substance of love as a source of confidence in the storm of my life.

As I floated in and out of the illusive secret place of peace, life was contemplated. The imagination was stretched to know all that was possible in a difficult time. If all was designed to break, I already felt broken ten times over, in a million pieces each. Was there still a remnant of the self holding out that needed removed? Was all that was happening designed to test the heart? Was there more humbling needed? Pleas for the pressure to end continued in waves as the heart was searched to find the whisper of joy through a revelation that would capture and explain the intense conditions of the times. No relief nor answers were anywhere near.

In the struggle to maintain zero, I found myself looking hard at the lives of the thousands of brothers all around. There are so many lost. So many beautiful people with wonderful characters, simply lost in the whirlwind of this world that entices them to be so far from who they truly are. From the very first day of entering the federal detention facility, many opportunities to edify a wide variety of characters, young and old, straight and gay alike, have happened. Through it all I have lived life being true to the heart and have simply related the inward journey of heart and faith to everyone. The search has been far and wide throughout the years for meaning and purpose, through the different ideals and ideas of the world and in human relationships and have only ended up empty and hurt. And now, a joy has been finally found that fulfills and challenges, too. Seeing testimony of Jesus is life, my love affair that brings great meaning but also stretches everything that the heart is about.

"Father, Father, why have you forsaken me?"

Jesus Christ

With the jury still out deliberating, peace was hard to find, comfort nowhere near, and I felt so far off in the distance of nowhere, very alone, like nobody cared as to what happened to Christopher Ibanez, that he could spend the rest of his life in the dungeon of steel and nobody would even take notice. No one to call, to speak with, or simply to be near, no one. As I reflected on life and all that has happened, a million questions emerged. How could this person do that, and that person this? Who am I to think I am special? Where is God? What is He up to? Why am I being left alone? Father, why have you forsaken me, I pleaded. To even think this was so faithless and convicting, and then the Lord astonishes and intrigues. There, at the bottom of the page of my opened journal are the words, "I will not forget you! See, I have engraved you on the palms of My hands"(Isaiah 49:15-16). I wept! The Lord knew what I needed to hear at the exact time that the faithless and convicting words were wrote asking the Lord why He has forsaken me. I cried, pleading not for the pressure to be removed but to forgive my faithless heart, for not believing, not trusting Him.

"It is finished."

Jesus Christ

Reflecting on all that has happened in the last five years, I easily recognize the subtlety of evil that lurked and encroached, that wanted my heart, that wanted me to forever stay in a dungeon, a prison of physical and spiritual realities. I think of the witnesses called to testify, some of which were very close, and the witnesses in the background that tried to trick and entrap, that wanted blood. I think of my lawyer who played both sides of the coin of justice. I thought of the chief investigator, the top cop, and how he fabricated evidence in many instances and used everyone around to try and obtain incriminating evidence. I thought of the prosecutor who cared not about truth but conviction, and the army of assistant district attorneys sitting at the prosecution table--scary! I felt betrayed in the most personal sense because all were doing whatever it took to advance wrong, bastardizing the very nature of who we are as beautiful people. This was the world of evil piled on high and thick, and then I thought of Jesus in the garden of Gethsemane, praying as blood sweat trickled down His face. This was intense, the weight of all sin upon Him, upon innocence, an intensity that compares to nothing anybody will know or experience. The world was on the Lord, my sins and that of humanity was on Him. And during the trial, the weight of my life and all that I have done, was upon me. My faith was stretched like no other time. This was the most intense life experience. My heart and life, and my future, were fully surrendered to the Lord. I was finished!

And then, on February 29th, 2016, at 2:27pm, a text message went out to my angel Peanuts from my lawyer, the jury had reached a verdict! Not guilty, not guilty, not guilty, twelve times over each juror spoke! A show of glory, of majestic power, shining brightly with love amid a surrounding army of darkness and nothing came close to touching a heart that embraced love. The sea of darkness was parted. I was overwhelmed. And every juror, young and old, male and female alike, had eyes that were tear-filled and flowing freely as I thanked each one. It was surreal, a fruit-filled time from my faith, hope and love of Jesus Christ.

At the federal detention center, as personal belongings were being packed after two years, hundreds of brothers gathered around. In tears, I hugged them and expressed gratitude for being family. All clapped as the iron-bar doors were opened, a rare sight in a federal judicial system that has a 98.1% conviction rate--nobody walks out free and clear. A miracle indeed. As the hand-clapping grew louder, the brothers in all four dormitory ranges gathered, giving a standing ovation as each were high-fived and hugged all the way out the front door of the house of steel, far

different then the rear basement door entered two years before. Outside the building, the steel home for two amazing and beautiful years, my angel Peanuts warmly greets me. We hugged and as we drove off she said my lawyer warned to watch for this and that. As more than fifteen traffic signals were passed, all of which were green, I said, "There are nothing but green lights down this road. If God is for us, who dare be against us!" The armies of the United States justice department had just been defied, a sea of darkness had just been parted, and the doors of the house of steel had been open forever.

Case 3:14-cr-00225-MMA Document 363 Filed 02/29/16 Page 1 of 1

FILED

FEB 29 2016

CLERK, U.S. DISTRICT COURT
SOUTHERN DISTRICT OF CALIFORNIA
BY DEPUTY

UNITED STATES DISTRICT COURT
SOUTHERN DISTRICT OF CALIFORNIA

UNITED STATES OF AMERICA,
Plaintiff,
v.
CHRISTOPHER STUPHIN IBANEZ,
Defendant.

Case No.: 14CR225-MMA

VERDICT

We the jury in the above entitled cause find the defendant Christopher Stuphin Ibanez: Not Guilty (Not Guilty/Guilty) of Conspiracy to Distribute Methamphetamine as charged in the indictment.

If you find the defendant guilty, do you further find unanimously beyond a reasonable doubt that the amount of methamphetamine the defendant conspired to distribute was more than 50 grams of actual methamphetamine?

____YES ____NO

Date: 2/29/16
San Diego, California

Foreperson of the Jury

Figure 5: Jury Verdict Sheet

Figure 6: Lawyer Joseph McMullen and I in his office upon release from the Federal Metropolitan Correctional Center (MCC) in downtown San Diego which is the tall building that can be seen directly left in the background of the photo.

Figure 7: I. Flores, aka "Peanuts." The artist behind the artwork and design of the book, a fellow minister, and love machine. Generously giving and always bringing a word from the Lord.

Figure 8: A hand-drawn picture of several of the brothers in the house of steel, all of us having a mischievous heathen side that surfaced every now and then. Freddy (front left) is the jailhouse barber, artist and tattoo specialist. I am shown at the upper right with food tray and cleaning spray bottle.

Figure 9: Peanuts' vision of "A Prisoner."

17

"For my own sake, for my own sake, I do this. How can I let myself be defamed? I will not yield my glory to another."

God

The Friday after closing arguments in the criminal case, I remember laughing and crying, grumbling to God, telling Him that the humor with which He was using was not funny, at all. The jury left for the weekend, to return on Monday the 29th of February, 2016, for further deliberations in the case. This was an intense time, the deck was stacked against me and I stood to be found guilty, and then the significance of the date dawns on me. The Lord, through the whole ordeal, spoke many times through the 9:11 numerical pattern at peculiar times. When the significance of February 29th(11), 2016(9), was realized, I smiled, cried, and grumbled to God, telling Him that this was not funny. God thought otherwise about His Divine sense of humor. My imagination saw Him, sitting on His throne with angels joyfully singing around Him, smiling while I laughed and cried, having a hard time trusting in His promise to rescue me. And rescue me He did!

The whole process of the trial had to play out as it did. Everything, the whole network of liars, lies, and deceptive devices of evil had to challenge a sincere heart, and I had to remain silent and still without defense because the Lord wanted my heart fully surrendered to Him and to leave no doubt in anybody's heart that it was God that made the not guilty verdict happen and who parted the sea of darkness and allowed passage through, while lies and evil were consumed by Truth. There was only one verdict of guilt in the courtroom, and that went to all who went against Truth, to all who deny that God's presence is in everything, and to all who refuse to listen to the voice of Jesus who calls all in love!

There have been many paths in the journey where focus has been lost, sight blinded by the race for meaningless ideas of wealth that only exemplified a void in life and increased emptiness and pain. But through it all I have remained true to my heart, and all has served to correct and refine, to recognize a Beauty. As such, all that has happened is profoundly meaningful. The heart has been shaken and shattered, stripped of all that has enslaved, and a beauty discovered, a love that runs deep in the fabric of all life. There is nothing more intriguing and captivating than being given a personal revelation by an all-powerful God. Chasing this treasure is a beauty that compares to nothing in all the world. It is the substance that makes life, far from what money and possessions offer. It is a treasure that unfolds with profound meaning and an indescribable joy and beauty.

Without the euphoria of drugs and the clouds of sin that were once a part of life for so long, messages can be seen all over, Divine communication speaking of how deeply the Lord loves all, implanted capsules of love that time contains, for all to see and hear if that is the desire of the heart. Whether in architecture, great literature, nature, art, people, the Bible, everything speaks forth a message of Love and Promise just waiting to be discovered by a sincere heart ready to commit. Every new revelation brings an explosive excitement that cannot be contained and must be told so all will fall in love with the Beautiful

that put it there.

"Write down the revelation and make it plain on tablets so that a herald may run with it."

Habakkuk, The Prophet

The heart has been captivated, even intrigued, by the many unusual and peculiar events that have happened, and intuition undoubtedly says these are "signs and wonders" of the Divine that court and bring great joy amid trial, challenge, and affliction. The most amazing discovery of the Lord is that He is surprisingly personal, involved and attentive in the littlest details, and understanding of my nature very humanly. God is very approachable. The majesty and veil into the presence of the all-powerful nature of the Divine is surprisingly simple to enter, and the trust and bond easily restored and instead of fear, love unfolds. Why else would the Lord reveal His handwriting and signature in everyday life other than to let us hear a voice to love and trust and find life. The Lord is simple, and therefore faith should be simple, too. There is a compelling to write about the simplicity of faith, to inspire the wondering of hearts to pass through the veil in truth and see how human-like an all-powerful and majestic God can be through the simple act of trust and surrender. It is mind-blowing how simple

faith is.

The last five years have been a Mount Everest of challenge. Every front that is important in life has become a gigantic mountain to scale. The law has been relentless. From friends to family and on through to lawyer and cellmates, the law, Blue-Shoes, has used all venues to fanatically pursue with every tool in the black bag of tricks. And pick and ax have dug and chopped through everything to find the golden nugget that will convict and have my name and steel cage number for the next twenty years. And nothing has kept me in chains! With an arrest for drug distribution, convicted or not, however, I will not be able to pump gas, dig a tar pit, clean a septic tank, or crush rocks into sand using a spoon as a means of meaningful employment. At this point, even riding a bicycle seems impossible with the amount of speeding tickets more than 100mph on the record.

At the age of fourteen, kicked out and expelled from school, a counselor asked what a dream profession would be. A professional racecar driver was the whole-hearted reply. Cars have been crashed and rolled over in all manner and fashion, and my neck broken. Cars have just not been professionally raced. Cars have been driven back and forth to work on icy roads in the American mid-west for twenty years and never once skidded or fish-tailed. And the only time in the last 150 years that it snows in Modesto, California, I happened to be the lucky one who drives over the ice and flips the car over on a perfectly straight road and breaks his neck! And do not ever ask a teenage daughter how she flipped her brand-new car over on a perfectly straight road because she will ask the same question many years in the future while you are strapped on a gurney with a broken neck from flipping a car over on a perfectly straight road! Experience speaks here--A crazy daughter. She had to have gotten this from her mother! That is my story, and I am sticking to it!

As for friends, there are none. All of them have betrayed and scattered except for a special one, Peanuts my angel. The Lord has given us a very special connection. Through thick and thin she has been there, making sure to visit me in the house of steel always, providing resources generously, and being a personal source of edification in life and faith. Many miracles have happened with her from beginning to present moments. Our connection is open and free, without shame. At one point my right testicle was hurting so bad that I told her about it and without saying anything she prayed and it was instantly healed. I was amazed at this. She, laughing hysterically! My cheerleader, my prayer warrior, and my dear friend whose smile of pure love when we first met has been the single most thing that has affected my faith thus far. It is a privilege and honor to know and love her.

My heart is wide open and transparent, given unconditionally, and Lord Jesus astonishing and leaving me awestruck. Anybody watching has seen for themselves that there are no games, no tricks, nothing but a desire for truth and Jesus revealing Himself for all to see. Signs and wonders occurring in individual lives repeatedly, leaving me in wonder why it took so long to notice and why I stand the only one wide-eyed and over-joyed. Faith is full of substance, the mind renewed, and the trumpet of Jesus Christ is blown for the world to hear, to call attention to evidence of the Divine that riddles the landscape of time, nature, and everyday life. The voice of the Lord speaks, are we listening?

Leaving the house of steel is bitter-sweet, for there are many hurting deeply and held captive by fear. There will never be joy in this, for these are my brothers, my family. This is heartache. The lost, the challenged and afflicted, are the body of Christ, and we must partake and feed all with love. In our homes and those of our neighbors, in our towns and on city sidewalks, in church and school dormitories, there is unimaginable pain and suffering, burdens and afflictions, bondages and sin, hidden behind the many fake personas we put on for others to see. From sexual abuse to incestuous relations to violence and murder, and addictions of all types, have touched our lives in one form or another whether we know it or not. It is there, testifying if only we choose to look and therefore see, see it being worn on the many faces and forms in life. Accessing hurting people happens through a sincere heart, authentic and true. Sharing in burdens then becomes a privilege to be honored and held in confidence. Love is the confidence and place of access, where life can be shared in a very personal way, and passage to freedom from the prisons of the heart can be shown. This is the gift of Love, a gift given by the Divine, one that gave me an honor to enter the hearts of many brothers in the house of steel. There is great treasure and privilege to share time with another, to create beautiful life moments and meaningful memories of love that are timeless. The richness of any human encounter will not be lost if we see people through the focus of love, where there are no faults only love that perfects all.

Moses had the privilege and honor to turn

around and see the "burning bush" and speak with God. I, in gratefulness, can look back in my life, upon the same ground that Moses stood, with the same intrigue, intensity, and beauty, and can see how Lord Jesus has been there every step of the way, speaking through the many wonders of His creation, sometimes with great humor, sometimes as a Spirit of rebuke, and sometimes with a supernatural presence. With the Lord, there are no sad stories or bad endings, only happy, joyful, and beautiful ones. Yes, there were many horrors in my life, given as a real picture of a person, with a struggle not to understand problems but life.

Two years in the house of steel proved to be the most beautiful time of my fifty-two years of life. This was an amazing time, an amazing adventure, and an amazing journey through the dungeon of cold and very imposing steel. Love gave this beauty. My emergency Jesus9:11 call to the Lord, to save me from a life that I did not know how to get out of, was answered with a comfort and gentle embrace. And the turbulent waters of the times, the calls of crystal-meth and the seductress Babylonia, all began to be stilled as all the gods in my heart were hard removed. I have learned to get out of the way, and let the Lord open the doors He wants me to go through, to allow Him to protect and guide while I simply love and trust Him and live my heart out in this life. Jesus Christ calls all, to trust Him for and with life. This is all I have done amidst chaos, struggle, and crazy.

We are all individual and unique, so we need simply to love the Lord with the whole heart in our own special way. Walk into Jesus presence without any preconceptions or ideas of how it should be and allow the Lord to provide His counsel and consolation. He is God, He knows everything and everybody, so let Him be God, the only God in life. Let the motivation simply be to know Him, and He will provide the adventure of amazing love that will capture and captivate every desire of the heart like nothing in this world can. And whether this book makes the New York Times bestseller list or flops in the gutter of nowhere land and reaches no one, the grand commissioning of my heart and life remains profoundly deep, for Jesus Christ has touched me in a very special way and has the allegiance of my heart forever. And this is my call, that everyone be touched, too, by the Lord no matter the fragile and broken condition or how deep in the pit of shame one may or may not find themselves. Just go to the Lord and find gentle love and discover transforming power. The Lord is one reach, one step, one thought back into His heart. He awaits with a love like nothing in this world or the riches in this life can offer. It is beautiful. It is freedom.

There are just so many things I want to tell the world that I could go on for a thousand years and still fail to capture the amazing that the Lord has made happen, that testifies to just how beautiful life is even amidst great challenge and struggle. Nothing held me captive no more, no bars of iron, no sin or shame, no substance or treasure of this world. Love captivated me, and Love set me free.

Life is short. We do not want to live in regret and lost possibility while life speeds away. We must all align with destiny now, walk. Every step of the way, a Voice will speak, and a wonder and sign will be shown, and the heart will be captivated and intrigued as the song of Truth begins to free the heart from the bonds of slavery that weigh life down. And the dawn of a new day will emerge and the essence of life will captivate in a way never known. As the inner journey of healing and reconciliation unfolds, the Lord opens new doors as He fills every newly discovered inner fold of the heart with love, a love that darkness flees from, a love that removes the veils of time and space and reveals individual destiny.

A free man, I walk the city sidewalks and surf

social networks and see circles created not through the embrace of love but by division. This is appalling. The passion with which this statement is made carries a hypocrisy, and it is recognized. But what will never be appreciated or accepted is what my eyes show of the world. We are better than this and fail to see our beauty. No longer do we appreciate each other as beautiful, individual creatures in a shared journey in the life experience. Instead, we look at each other in judgment! We look down on the homeless, the tattooed individual, the neighbor with the rundown car and messy yard, and only extend invitations to our homes and churches to those that are similar and liked, the elite, rather than to all with equal eyes on the same plane of love. One must wonder the direction that we now travel. We recognize the big red nose of our neighbor and fail to see we have one of our own that may be even more pronounced!

After excusing herself, a homeless lady sat on the ground beside the table that I was sitting at one morning at a coffee shop, saying she was making a movie and was acting out a part. She then began yelling, "Everybody is an actor, and Angelina Jolie is carrying stolen art and Becky's big red nose is ugly." Turning to face her, I intently listened while everyone around looked down at her while running off. Her satire went right over everybody's head. She was speaking to all that looked down on her with hate and judgmental eyes and not looking upon the self that is hidden behind the fake persona's worn for all to see. Life is a movie and we have a choice to be actors or artists. As actors, there is conformity to and allegiance with groups that we identify with and share the same ideals in social spheres and look down upon all other groups. And we wear fake personas to hide our big red noses and think because of status, social standing or large bank accounts we are better than the next person, like someone dirty and homeless. Because these are fake persona's hidden behind, it is stolen art, not who we are. If we are artists, we recognize our own condition, our big and ugly red noses, and live according to who we are and share time and opportunity in the journey, in the experience, of life. Not with hate, contempt, or malice in our heart, but with love and recognition of each other's pain and fallible nature and see big red noses as existential art that brings beauty and flavor to the landscape and different fields of life. And we bring moments of joy, and smiles, through extending acts and gestures of kindness however they may be to reach across boundaries, to the rich and poor alike, the well to do or the depressed, the high-class, the low-class, and even the no-class.

While sitting at a public aid office waiting to apply for assistance after being released from the house of steel, the day was somewhat reflected upon, the people seen and the questions being asked during the interview process. The lady doing the interview made me feel very comfortable. I felt embarrassed and ashamed and began giving her an excuse for applying, like I had a more legitimate excuse then the rest because I had been federally detained and exonerated from all criminal charges. How judgmental to think my excuse was worthier. I did not need an excuse and the attendant made it clear that she was not there to judge but to help. How could I then judge anyone else's circumstances, whether good or bad? Who was I to think that I had a special story, that my circumstances were worthier and different from the rest? No, I was a criminal who had to be saved from a past that came haunting. I do not have a unique story, I have a remarkable gift of faith that a remarkable God gave. I am just an ordinary guy, like everyone else, who at one time did not know who he was and entangled himself in the search of his heart.

My heart has been found and is offered to the reader, in the hope that the imagination is captured and the heart intrigued through the story of my struggles and the journey of my deliverance. I have nothing but a grateful heart and a beautiful life that the Lord has given back. I put my heart into this book

and filled it with love that will hopefully touch even a tiny area of the heart. And therefore, it is hoped that the heart of the reader has been fed, to inspire hope and embrace the call of life from the heart of Jesus Christ, the call of love, that is free and full of meaning, away from a world that always leaves us empty inside. May my story abundantly bless you, and through it find the love the Lord has for you and cherish it like no other in your life. May you taste the Lord and know that He is not only good, but so very beautiful. Let Him intrigue and captivate you in the adventure of life and love. Lord Jesus be with you, bring you peace, and may His love transform you.

I had an amazing journey.

"But these are written that you may believe that Jesus is the Messiah, the son of God, and that by believing you may have life in his name."

John, The Son of Thunder

"Whatever you do, work at it with all your heart, as working for the Lord, not for human masters."

The Apostle Paul

"Whatever your hands find to do, do it with all your might, for in the realm of the dead, where you are going, there is neither working nor planning nor knowledge nor wisdom."

King Solomon

Figure 10: "Peanuts" by M.S. Koppel

Figure 11: "Chris" by Christie Koppel

Faith
Love

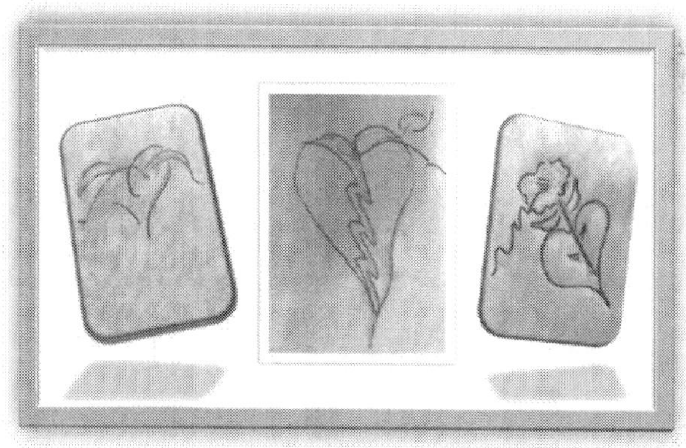

TRUTh

CIBANEZ911@GMAIL.COM

Endnotes

---

[i] Kramarik, Akiane. *"Love."*
[ii] Allen, James. *"As a Man Thinketh."* The Savory Publishing Company. 1903
[iii] Kramarik, Akiane. *"Wisdom."*
[iv] Angelou, Maya. United States postage stamp quote
[v] Batterson, Mark. Writing Your History. *Influence Magazine*
[vi] Schulz, Gregory P. *"The Problem of Suffering: A Father's Hope."* Concordia Publishing House, 2011

Made in the USA
San Bernardino, CA
14 December 2018